Body
Psychotherapy
for the 21st
Century

Nick Totton

Body Psychotherapy for the 21st Century

CONFER
BOOKS

Published in 2020 by Confer Books, London

www.confer.uk.com

Registered office:
21 California, Martlesham, Woodbridge, Suffolk IP12 4DE, England

3 5 7 9 10 8 6 4

This is a work of nonfiction. Any similarity between the characters and situations
within its pages, and places, persons, or animals living or dead, could be
unintentional and co-incidental. Some names and identifying details have been
changed or omitted to, in part, protect the privacy of individuals.

British Library Cataloguing in Publication Data. A catalogue record for this book is
available from the British Library.

ISBN: 978-1-913494-04-9 (paperback)
ISBN: 978-1-913494-05-6 (ebook)

Typeset by Bespoke Publishing Ltd.
Printed in the UK by Ashford Colour Press

Contents

INTRODUCTION 1

CHAPTER 1 25

CHAPTER 2 65

CHAPTER 3 93

CHAPTER 4 132

REFERENCES 151

INDEX 158

INTRODUCTION

The first thing to say about body psychotherapy, perhaps, is that it's not a very helpful name. It is the name we have, and it would probably be impractical to change it; but it seems to imply that BP (an abbreviation I will often use) is *solely* about working with the body, rather than any of the other things that psychotherapy involves. Also, it is rather contradictory, or at least paradoxical: since the "psycho" in psychotherapy refers to psyche – spirit or mind – body psychotherapy literally means "mind healing for the body".

Perhaps this mixing up of mind and body actually does reflect something real about body psychotherapy: that it questions the neat dualistic separation between these two categories that is often referred to as "Cartesian", and that has dominated Western culture for centuries. BP comes from a very different perspective that ultimately leads to treating "body" and "mind" as two complementary facets of a single whole, in which all consciousness is embodied, and every living body is (capable of being) conscious.

This way of thinking does not fit easily into ordinary language, which is deeply permeated by dualistic attitudes towards many aspects of reality, and perhaps in particular towards mind and body, psyche and soma. One way in which body psychotherapy addresses this problem is, instead of speaking about bodies and minds, to introduce the term "bodymind", or even "bodymindspirit". Another way is to move, as many people in the field have been doing, towards emphasising the concept of *embodiment*.

Embodiment is a double term, meaning both the *state* of being a self-aware organism, something that all living human beings share, and also the meta-level *process* of realising and experiencing that we are a self-aware organism. This process is one in which we are all involved, but that varies in degree between individuals and situations. So this sense of embodiment means the moment-by-moment experience of our existence as living bodies, with all the joy and grief, pleasure and pain, power and vulnerability which that involves; and a commitment to exploring "the organismic aspect of our being, without which we cannot exist but which we always have difficulty fully accepting" (Totton, 2015, Ch. 1).

Embodiment challenges us to own and integrate the various woundings we encounter in life, rather than leaving them frozen in patterns of bodily tension and avoidance that create a local numbing in our awareness and sensitivity. The reality for each of us will always be a set of compromises, as our embodiment finds ways to make the best of its situation, to preserve as much freedom and flexibility as possible while also protecting us from threat.

This, I think, is a summary of a way of understanding things with which most body psychotherapists would probably roughly agree. The job of body psychotherapy then emerges as one of supporting clients in recognising and re-evaluating the conscious and unconscious embodied choices that they have made, and opening up new opportunities for relating to the world, to themselves, and to others.

FOUR MODELS

Despite body psychotherapists' rough agreement on the task, they have still developed many different ways of working: schools and modalities proliferate within BP at least as much as they do within psychotherapy in general. To help find a way through this tangle of approaches, in an earlier book (Totton, 2003) I identified three core models for body psychotherapy. Much has happened in the field since then, so that I now need to add a fourth. I think these models can clearly be observed in use, but often without much clarity about how they relate to and in some ways contradict each other. I call them the *Adjustment* model, the *Trauma/Discharge* model, the *Process* model, and – the recent addition – the *Relational* model. They cut across the boundaries between schools: often all four can be discovered in any given approach, in varying proportions and with varying emphases. I offer them as a tool for grasping and analysing the similarities and differences of schools of body psychotherapy.

Adjustment

This fits least well into psychotherapy, and many feel it should be relegated to the realm of body-work proper where it originated – approaches like massage, yoga, and so on where adjustment and correction are entirely legitimate concepts. The model treats therapy as *corrective*, reorganising and realigning the body to fit a definite norm and thus, it believes, restoring the mind to a healthy and desirable condition. Alexander Lowen writes: "A person's emotional life depends on the motility of his [sic] body, which in turn is a function of the flow of excitation throughout it. Disturbances of this flow occur as blocks" (1975, p. 53). By removing these blocks and undamming energy, one restores the patient to their healthy "first nature", as opposed to the "second nature" of neurosis (Lowen, 1975, p. 107).

This model has major limitations. It can be used to crudely privilege soma over psyche, claiming that one should always work from the body to the mind. It also devalues the complex protective and expressive functions of bodily "dysfunctions", where states of high or low tension can be the best available defences for a threatened sense of self – a realisation that is a major contribution of the "second wave" of BP. It has little room for phenomena like internal conflict and ambivalence. And it assumes the practitioner's superior understanding of what the client needs, and her right to apply that understanding to the client's body – literally "manipulating" them on a bodily level.

Every time we say "normal" or "healthy" – and we do say them, however much we theoretically disapprove – we are using the Adjustment model; it is deeply embedded in BP traditions. Many see it as an outmoded relic, which should be abolished;

I used to agree. I now believe we need to respect the persistence, in body psychotherapy, and in psychotherapy generally, of the idea of "cure": an idea that will not go away. Taking the body seriously, we cannot easily ignore its wish for healing – the client's body wishing to receive it, and the therapist's body wishing to offer it.

Every therapist surely has strong notions of good functioning, ideas that constitute their categories of perception. This is amplified in body psychotherapists, trained to respond sensitively to styles of embodiment: inevitably we experience some bodies as enjoyable and positive, others as unpleasant and negative. Like everyone, we have a strong tendency to fit our experience into binary models (Totton, 2011, pp. 12–13). Hence we need urgently to cultivate a critical awareness of our judgements, and steadily extend our acceptance of different styles of embodiment. The traditional Adjustment model can all too easily be used to denigrate many kinds of difference from the mainstream, including sexuality, gender, and "abledness".

An example of an Adjustment-based BP session: John has been coming for sessions with Douglas for some time, and they have been working on his "ungroundedness" – a stiffness and weakness in his legs, and a lack of connection with his feet, which they have associated with his difficulty in "standing his ground" in the world. Today, Douglas invites John to adopt a stress position – knees slightly bent, but pushing up from the ground into his sacrum, and breathing deeply "into his legs", that is, imagining the energy of his breath going into them and focusing his awareness on their small in-and-out movement accompanying each breath. "Stay with it," Douglas encourages him, "keep breathing and feel the stretch." The posture becomes increasingly painful, but John has learnt to recognise this as a "good pain". After a few minutes his legs start to tremble with increasing force. "OK," Douglas says, "that's great, now gradually relax, come out of it and see how it feels." For a while John stands, letting his breath move of its own accord, and enjoying a pleasurable tingling sensation in his legs, feet, and pelvis. He feels relaxed, empowered, and in command, and experience tells him that this will transfer into his life outside the session.

Trauma/Discharge

This powerful theory of traumatic shock and reparative emotional discharge was first formulated in modern terms by Freud and Breuer (1895d), and is currently very popular in psychotherapy. Freud repeatedly describes an external trauma which he characterises as a "foreign body", like a splinter or a parasite, entering and attacking the child's bodymind so that it must adapt and shape itself around it (Freud, 1926d; Totton, 2002).

Although Reich does not speak of the "foreign body", it underlies his conceptualisation of repression, aggression, and resistance. For Reich, our deepest resistance is against surrender and spontaneity: trauma leads us to experience *our own body* as "foreign" – it seems vital to suppress feeling and emotional expression so as to avoid being overwhelmed, but this can only be achieved by alienating ourselves from our bodies and "senselessly defend[ing ourselves] against the cherished capacity for pleasure" (Reich, 1973, p. 336). Chronic trauma leads to *dissociation* – splitting between different systems, for example feeling and thinking, or different circuits of memory.

If the ruling metaphor of the Adjustment model is straightening a crooked limb, that of the Trauma/Discharge model is expelling a splinter that has created painful inflammation around itself. Usually the body itself does this; and the Trauma/Discharge model sees the practitioner's role as supporting and encouraging a natural healing. The Discharge part of the model expects this healing to occur through emotional abreaction, the release and full conscious expression of emotions "locked into" rigid musculature.

It is now widely agreed that intense abreaction is only helpful within a strong therapeutic container, and that for certain personality structures it may be damaging. Many body psychotherapists use a gentler, more gradual approach, avoiding "retraumatising" the client, and focusing on supporting their strength and competence – managing and integrating the traumatic experience rather than reliving it. But most remain convinced that "post-traumatic symptoms are, fundamentally, incomplete physiological responses suspended in fear", that "will not go away until the responses are discharged and completed" (Levine, 1997, p. 34; cf. Rothschild, 2000, who shifts the emphasis further from "discharge" to "completion"). There are other approaches not directly within body psychotherapy, like Eye Movement Desensitisation and Reprocessing (EMDR) and Emotional Freedom Technique (EFT), whose practitioners believe we can let go of trauma without having to re-experience it.

Trauma/Discharge is an excellent tool for approaching specific psychological wounds – often conceptualised as "post-traumatic stress disorder" (PTSD). But, again, it has several limitations. It often does not consider how therapy can itself potentially *replicate* trauma, in ways that can be harmful or useful or both (Ferenczi, 1933), but tends to assume the therapist's role as friend and ally. It often focuses on grossly traumatic events, and perhaps not enough on the universal, subcritical trauma of socialisation. And the model often does not address the complex questions trauma work raises about fantasy and reality and how elements of each become entangled with the other, but can assume a too simple one-to-one relationship between the client's experience and what has historically occurred.

An example of a Trauma/Discharge-based BP session: Gill comes for her regular session with her therapist, Sarah, who notices as soon as she comes into the room that her shoulders are tight and high. She feeds this back to Gill, who says, "Yes, now you mention it I can sense that." She works her shoulders for a minute, but reports, "No, they won't let go – they don't want to let go." With permission, Sarah stands behind Gill's chair and uses her thumbs to press hard on sensitive points in Gill's shoulders. Acting into a role, she commands Gill, "Let go! You have to let go!" Gill is used to this way of working, and responds: "No, I won't. I don't want to." As Sarah's thumbs press deeper into the sore muscles, Gill starts to breathe deeply and to yell – "No! NO! LEAVE ME ALONE! I DON'T WANT TO!!" and shakes off Sarah's grip. She cries deeply while Sarah very gently holds her shoulders, which are now soft and yielding. Sarah sits down in her chair again, and they talk about Gill's experience of childhood sexual abuse, already shared in earlier sessions, and about a current situation which has brought back feelings from the abuse.

Process
The third model takes the idea of supporting a natural healing process even further – in its pure form it drops the idea of "healing" entirely, along with the idea of anything being wrong.

> *If you want to help someone ... turn the person inward towards experience. Don't turn them inward for explanations. Don't ask them why they feel that way – you're*

wrecking the process right there. ... Don't
ask for explanations. You don't need them.
You don't need anything. ... Just turn them
inwards towards their experience. You
don't need to understand a thing.
(Kurtz, 1985, pp. ii–iii)

Using this model, a therapist allows the client's bodymind to act rather than be acted on, and to generate motifs freely and playfully. The ruling metaphor here is perhaps a river that, once undammed, flows powerfully to the sea. In the therapy session one aims to let go of theory, and any concept of fixed states or entities. "Our bodies are us as process, not as a thing. Structure is slowed-down process" (Keleman, 1975, p. 66). A great strength of this is that it avoids privileging the therapist's version of reality, health, and normality that I discussed above. It assumes that trauma and misadjustment will self-repair given any opportunity, and that the most apparently bizarre behaviour can be part of this process. This resembles the concept of "unwinding" in craniosacral therapy (Cohen, 1995, p. 82).

Again there are limitations. Most process-centred body psychotherapies relate uneasily to *state*-based concepts like "character", "neurosis", etc. Fritz Perls, for example, insists that instead of trying to identify and treat "the 'real' underlying character that the therapist guesses at ... we need only help the patient develop his creative identity" (Perls, Hefferline, & Goodman, 1951, pp. 508–509), reflecting a fear of getting captured by the heavy gravitational field of state thinking, losing one's capacity to fly freely.

But states are what we mostly inhabit; and state and process are intertwined and complementary concepts, each making sense of and delineating the other (Totton & Jacobs, 2001, pp. 111–112). Just as a cell needs a surrounding membrane to define it, human beings need "edges" (Mindell, 1985) – psychological boundaries that resist change – as our grip on embodiment; while it may be helpful to move through any particular edge, we cannot do without edges altogether.

An example of a Process-based BP session: Philip is talking with his therapist Janet about his relationship with his husband. Janet notices that as he talks, Philip's head is moving in a noticeable and slightly unusual way. She points this out to him – which, as with many people, used at first to cause the movement to stop instantly – but Philip has got used to this approach, and lets the movement continue and develop into a sort of swooping, dipping curve. Janet makes appreciative sounds, and after a minute suggests that they stand up, and that Philip continue the movement and bring his whole body into it. He starts to swoop and dip around the room, with his arms spontaneously coming out from his side; Janet joins him, and for a minute or so they both angle and curve around the room. "Is there a sound?" Janet asks, and Philip starts to make a mournful, warbling hoot that seems to correspond to the movement. Janet hoots back, and soon the dance seems to reach a natural conclusion. They remain standing, and Janet says, "I had the sense that we were birds, is that right?" Philip nods. "Yes,

I felt like a sad, lonely bird looking for its nest."
"Does that connect with what you were saying
about your husband?" Janet asks.

Relational
It is fitting that this model has an adjective rather
than a noun as its name, since it maintains Reich's
emphasis on *the way in which* clients do or say
things rather than *what* they do or say. Reading
Reich's case histories we can see his constant alertness to the relational content of his clients' style
of speech and expression, and the powerful use
he makes of it.

The model treats embodied relating as the
ground of all psychotherapy, including talking
therapy (Totton, 2015). It attends closely to the
impact that the client's and therapist's bodies
have on each other, how bodies can cue each other into following an interactional script learnt in
early life. Many of us notice how differently we
act and experience ourselves with different clients.
The relational model offers a way to think deeply

about these differences, and to make use of the responses that we track in our own bodies to shape and direct the work. The ruling metaphor might be an improvised dance where neither of the couple leads, but the pattern is co-constructed.

An example of a Relational-based BP session: Indra is working with Elaine, a fairly new client whom she has seen half a dozen times. The work has been going quite well, but Indra is aware of Elaine's reserve, and wondering whether this is just an initial position or something more deep-rooted. As they talk about various events in Elaine's week, Indra scans her own body state, something she habitually does while with clients; she becomes aware of a sensation of heat in her throat and chest. She encourages this experience to grow by focusing some of her attention on it, and it starts to feel like a red-hot ball of fire – in fact, she finds herself beginning to sweat. While this is going on, Elaine is describing going out for the evening with a group of friends, and Indra realises that she is experiencing the way in which her client is talking as *cool*. Is the ball of fire in her chest a response to this coolness? It seems rather extreme! But then she realises that one of the friends Elaine was out with is the same person who, Elaine has said in a previous session, told a malicious story about her. "Did you ever sort out that situation with Malika?" she asks. "Well," Elaine says, "it seemed better to keep cool." "Did you really feel cool, though?" Indra says. "When I think about it and put myself in your place, I feel quite hot and bothered." Elaine looks put out and shrugs. "I try to be grown up about things," she says. "The trouble is that parts of us *aren't* grown up," Indra suggests; "but I have a feeling you don't like me saying that." Elaine sighs. "It's true," she admits, "I did feel cross with you for making me remember what Malika did." "That's OK," says Indra. "You"ll probably feel much crosser with me sometimes as we go on, and I want to hear about it."

The Relational model is necessarily relativist and constructivist in its approach; for example, it asks what effects using any of the four models, including this one, will have on how we present ourselves for relationship with clients – for the Adjustment model perhaps the skilled and detached expert; for the Trauma/Discharge model the provocateur/midwife; for the Process model the playful partner who may also be slippery and hard to pin down; and for the Relational model itself, the wounded and imperfect fellow human who is willing to put skin in the game and risk their own self-esteem. Each of these ways of relating will be useful with certain clients or at certain times, and not with others or at other times; and all of the above examples of imaginary sessions would be legitimate BP events – conceivably all four modalities could even appear within the same session. I will be saying more about the Relational model in Chapter 3.

WHAT FOLLOWS

This book is a short introduction to a rich and complex field, in which after 35 years' practice I naturally have considerable interest and investment: a mixed blessing, perhaps, since I am fascinated by details and intricacies that will be of little concern to someone coming to the subject for the first time. I have tried to balance the need for concision and straightforwardness with the need adequately to represent complexity, and at a minimum to avoid misleading the reader.

Introductory texts always raise problems of sequencing, where one passage will not be understood until another has been read, yet to put the second one first would be equally confusing for other reasons. So as not to interrupt the flow, some terms are not fully defined on their first appearance; explanations of many of these will be found in Chapter 3. However I would still encourage you to read the book more or less in sequence, because I think grasping the history of body psychotherapy greatly facilitates making sense of its theory and practice. But of course everyone will have their own preferences about how to read.

Chapter 1 outlines the development of BP from Freud onwards up to the 1990s, when what we may call, on the model of computer software, Body Psychotherapy 1.0 began to develop into Body Psychotherapy 2.0. Earlier editions have naturally not disappeared, but, as so often, continue to exist alongside later ones: some people are still using XP on their laptops. Chapter 2 gives an account of BP 2.0; Chapter 3 moves from a diachronic to a synchronic approach, focusing on the somewhat imaginary object, "body psychotherapy now". Chapter 4 then examines various debates and controversies, and peers into the future, or alternative futures, of the field.

At this point I want to express my gratitude to Rod Tweedy and Confer, for asking me to write this book; to the University of Edinburgh, for giving me access to its library as a visiting fellow; to Shoshi Asheri, Roz Carroll, Lidy Evertson, Helene Fletcher, and Emma Palmer, for reading and commenting on a draft (they of course have no responsibility for any errors, though they are collectively responsible for improving the whole); and to all my peers, colleagues, trainees, and clients, for their essential roles in my process of development as a therapist, teacher, and writer on the topic. Thank you.

SUGGESTED READING

For simplicity, only direct quotations or sources are referenced; however, at suitable points throughout the book, I offer suggestions for further relevant reading. The books below are general accounts, anthologies, or introductions, ending with four books each of which explores one of the BP models I have outlined above.

Marlock, G., & Weiss, H. (Eds.) (2016). *The Handbook of Body Psychotherapy and Somatic Psychology.* Berkeley, CA: North Atlantic.

Payne, H., Koch, S., & Tantia, J. (Eds.) (2019). *The Routledge International Handbook of Embodied Perspectives in Psychotherapy: Approaches from Dance Movement and Body Psychotherapies.* London: Routledge.

Staunton, T. (Ed.) (2002. *Body Psychotherapy*. London: Brunner-Routledge.

Totton, N. (2003). *Body Psychotherapy: An Introduction*. Maidenhead, UK: Open University Press.

Totton, N. (Ed.) (2005). *New Dimensions in Body Psychotherapy*. Maidenhead, UK: Open University Press.

Dychtwald, K. (1978). *Bodymind: A Synthesis of Eastern and Western Ways to Self-awareness, Health and Personal Growth*. London: Wildwood House.

Levine, P. A. (1997). *Waking the Tiger: Healing Trauma*. Berkeley, CA: North Atlantic.

Mindell, A. (1985). *River's Way: The Process Science of Dreambody*. London: Penguin Arkana.

Totton, N. (2015). *Embodied Relating: The Ground of Psychotherapy*. London: Karnac/Routledge.

HISTORY

Where should we begin a history of body psycho-therapy? We could justifiably go back a very long way: Richard Grossinger (1995) has shown there are clear similarities between shamanic practices and BP, with connections traceable in particular via mesmerism, while Michel Heller (2012) describes the roots of BP thinking in the whole Western philosophical tradition. (For both, see *Suggested Reading* at the end of the chapter.)

In a brief survey like this, however, it seems

appropriate to begin with the start of modern psychotherapy, where the "Big Four" of body psychotherapy are pretty clearly Sigmund Freud, Wilhelm Reich, Fritz Perls, and – surprisingly influential given that he did not work directly with the body – Carl Jung. We should note the limitation implied by the fact that these are all white males of central European ancestry.

I will focus in particular on the work of Wilhelm Reich, who first combined the fields of bodywork and psychotherapy, definitively shaping BP's main line of development. Reich was himself originally a psychoanalyst, and his approach was based in Freudian theory; however, he was also strongly indebted to other contemporary approaches to the body. We will look first at the psychoanalytic context, then at the field of bodywork.

FREUD AND PSYCHOANALYSIS

It is not often remembered that Freud's early path-breaking work was grounded in an active engagement with his clients' bodies. He used to spend "hours lying on the floor next to a person in a hysterical crisis" (Ferenczi, 1988, p. 93), and engage in "pinching", "pressing", and "kneading" a patient's legs, relieving someone else's stomach pain by stroking her and regularly massaging her whole body, and holding patients' heads with his hands to help them access memories (Freud & Breuer, 1895d, pp. 204–205, 106–110, 173–174). We even find this:

> *Yesterday Mrs K again sent for me because of cramplike pains in her chest; generally it has been because of headaches. In her case I have invented a strange therapy of my own: I search for sensitive areas, press on them, and thus provoke fits of shaking that free her.*
> (Quoted in Masson, 1985, p. 120)

This would fit right into a modern body psychotherapy session. However, it is never mentioned again in Freud's work or that of his followers, who move further and further away from this embodied approach in a way Bruce Barratt calls "body phobic", derived from "a fear-based conservatism" that expresses "our culturally endorsed alienation from our embodied experience" (Barratt, 2010, p. 79). As a theoretical system, though, psychoanalysis is irretrievably body-centred, describing how bodily impulses are taken up and transformed through their representation in the mind, and how problems arise from the confrontation of our bodily drives with opposing forces, both internal and external (Totton, 1998). For Freud, drives originate in bodily stimulus, and seek to remove the stimulus by satisfying it – like scratching an itch, as folk wisdom recognises. The bodily drives are the foundation on which the whole superstructure of psychoanalysis rests.

Freud stresses that the ego "is first and foremost a bodily ego", "ultimately derived from bodily sensations, chiefly from those springing from the surface of the body" (1923b, pp. 15, 16). He sees the ego as a psychological version of the *skin* – a protective organ giving shape and definition to the whole. Psychological problems stem from the inherent contradiction between the desires of the body and the requirements of civilisation, mediated to the individual child through their family and "bound into" the structure of the individual ego – that is, the structure of the individual body – by the policing of bodily acts like feeding, excretion, and masturbation. According to Freud this individual repression builds on a deep-rooted human difficulty in tolerating pleasure and spontaneity, which he concludes is probably innate.

Freud was not alone in interacting with his analysands' bodies. Sandor Ferenczi, perhaps Freud's most prominent colleague, found himself late in his career re-engaging with the physical body in ways that rather dismayed him – supporting and encouraging patients into altered states where they apparently relived and discharged forgotten traumatic experiences. These experiences led Ferenczi to break with Freudian orthodoxy, arguing that the despotic power of the practitioner to define and control the therapeutic situation was actually itself retraumatising – a very contemporary concern.

Another body-centred analyst, who originally developed his ideas independently of Freud, was Georg Groddeck, who traced virtually all human experience back to unconscious sexual impulses, and used intensive and painful massage to bring these to awareness: "[T]he patient's changing expressions reveal hidden secrets of his soul … Unconscious impulses … betray themselves in his involuntary movements" (1931, p. 236). Reich knew both Ferenczi and Groddeck, whose work later resurfaces within body psychotherapy.

BODYWORK TRADITIONS

Reich's psychoanalytic background led him to the body, but he was also strongly influenced by dance and movement practices popular in the early twentieth century, particularly in the German-speaking world where they were generally known as *Gymnastik*, and in Scandinavia. There was an enormous network of these techniques, among the best remembered of which are Eurhythmics, and Isadora Duncan's expressive "evolutionary" approach; many of them paid great attention to breathing, and many were linked to spiritual practices. A particularly influential figure was Elsa Gindler (1885–1961), whose importance for body psychotherapy has only recently been rediscovered.

Gindler belonged to a reform movement in gymnastics that aimed to move away from a precise external discipline to discovering the individual's inner rhythms and unique organismic expression. Through her students, she had an extraordinarily wide influence on later approaches, including Reichian therapy, Feldenkrais, Gestalt (Laura Perls was one of her pupils), and Bobath physiotherapy; several wives and partners of well-known therapists were among her followers. One of these was the dancer and choreographer Elsa Lindenberg, who became Reich's lover in Berlin in the early 1930s; but Reich was already familiar with Gindler's approach through his close friend Clare Fenichel, who was also her student, and his daughter Eva attended a "Gindler school".

It has been suggested that Lindenberg was "probably the person who taught Reich most of what he knew about working with the body" (Geuter, Heller, & Weaver, 2010, p. 66), following Eva Reich's view that he would not "have begun to work with the body, and especially the breath, if he had not been influenced by the Gindler method" (ibid., p. 65). This may underestimate the importance of Reich's allegiance to Freud's early theories; my own strong impression is that Reich learned about working with the body by doing it, starting out with a body-based variant of free association and gradually becoming more interventionist as he gained experience. He did not use standing movement at all in his approach, which was much closer to that of Ferenczi and Groddeck, both of whom he knew well.

Having said this, it is important to rediscover the role of this largely female network of bodyworkers in the early history of the field, and the following quotation makes Gindler's relevance to BP clear:

> *For her, breathing was a teacher: simply being attentive to it is a way of learning how things are with one, of learning what needs to change for fuller functioning – for more reactivity in breathing and thus in the whole person. She did not teach others what they "ought" to be, but only to find out how they were.*
> (Roche, quoted in Geuter, Heller, & Weaver, 2010, p. 63)

WILHELM REICH

In developing a body-centred psychoanalytic technique, Wilhelm Reich (1897–1957) regarded himself not as a rebel, but as carrying forward Freud's project of reconciling "mind" and "body" within the individual. Reich began taking analytic patients in 1920, while still a medical student and in his early twenties – young even for the time, though not uniquely so. Over the next decade he became an increasingly important figure in the new profession, taking a major role in developing clinical technique and group supervision. This led him to a consolidation and sharpening of analytic methods, and a developing focus on the body and bodily sexuality.

Reich's body-centred technique arose from investigating the real meaning of psychoanalytic concepts like repression. He shifted the emphasis from *what* the child represses to *how* the child represses, concluding that, just as libido and desire are for psychoanalysis ultimately bodily, biological phenomena, so repression – the force that opposes desire – is also bodily, manifesting in a habitual muscular rigidity that "represents the most essential part of the process of repression" (Reich, 1973, p. 300).

Very simply, if our childhood expressions of bodily need and desire – for example, reaching out to be picked up and carried, or wanting to suck the breast – are not welcomed, then the muscles expressing these needs, in these examples those of the arms and mouth, tighten up to prevent revealing something that will be met with punishment or rejection. Equally, and just as importantly, the anger, grief, or fear that is our natural response to rejection is *also* likely to be rejected; so again we tighten our body to repress our emotional expression, including limiting our breathing.

This is perhaps Reich's most important discovery, and the core of his concept of "functional identity": physical rigidity in the muscles and emotional rigidity in the psyche are simply different facets of a single phenomenon. Rather than Freud's "skin ego" described above, Reich identifies a "muscle ego", a pattern of bodily organisation that becomes the scaffolding for our whole personality. Hence he speaks in the same breath of "muscular armouring" and "character armouring" – parallel, interlocking ways of protecting our soft insides from the hard world. (I will say more about character in Chapter 3.)

For Reich, these new ways of seeing illuminated many problems of analytic work, which originally assumed that simply *explaining* how the patient's material revealed their unconscious desire would lead to transformation. He realised that words were not enough: unless the embodied patterns of the patient's resistance were addressed, verbal work could be largely ineffective. He therefore began to work on both his clients' character attitudes, and their muscular tension: as when opening a stiff drawer, working alternately on each side – the bodily and the psychological – often proved most effective.

Reich's initial bodywork was slow, painstaking, and uninvasive, a close equivalent to analytic free association, surely influenced by his senior colleague Ferenczi. He patiently and repeatedly encouraged clients to just breathe and let go to any spontaneous bodily phenomena – trembling, jerking, facial expressions, sounds, whatever manifested itself.

Often what emerged were thoughts, images, memories, feelings, and reactions to the therapist. To use a more contemporary language, Reich follows and supports his clients' process as it successively occupies different channels of experience, including bodily sensation and motor impulse, verbal and visual material, and the channel of relationship – the basic character attitude manifesting towards the therapist as love, hate, neediness, indifference, manipulation, arrogance, or whatever else. Reich's work implicitly develops Ferenczi's insight that the therapeutic relationship is critical in body-centred work.

As a committed social activist, Reich was always conscious of the social and political aspects of armouring, and how repression of energy and spontaneity acts to reinforce capitalist labour relations, by rendering people more dissociated, passive, and obedient. Hence he rejected the increasing emphasis in psychoanalysis on *internal* conflicts, and stressed the fundamental conflict between individual desire and external repression.

The psychic process reveals itself as the re-sult of the conflict between drive demand and the external frustration of this demand. Only secondarily does an internal conflict between desire and self-denial result from this initial opposition. … There are social, *more correctly, economic interests that cause such suppressions and repressions …* (Reich, 1972, p. 287)

Reich created projects to spread information on and access to sexual contact, birth control, and abortion among young people, eventually forming the "Sex-Pol" movement, a mass campaigning organisation that was supported by the Communist Party until the leadership decided it was too scandalous. Roughly simultaneously, Reich's sexual and social politics led to his rejection by both the Communists and the International Psychoanalytical Association.

It was primarily his position as an active communist – at a point when psychoanalysis was trying to achieve some sort of compromise with the Nazis – that left Reich excluded from the analytic movement. In the period during and immediately after his exclusion, however, institutional psychoanalysis shook off many of its more radical and body-centred themes. "Slowly but surely," as Reich wrote, "psychoanalysis was cleansed of all Freud's achievements" (Reich, 1973, p. 125). Sexuality became a psychological phenomenon divorced from the body – "something shadowy; the 'libido' concept was deprived of every trace of sexual content and became a figure of speech" (ibid., p. 124). Reich and the psychoanalytic mainstream began to move in opposite directions.

After his exclusion from psychoanalysis in 1934, Reich developed an independent approach to psychotherapy and to the study of life and nature, which eventually crystallised as "orgonomy". It would be fair to say that in his later years he steadily lost interest in psychotherapy as such, or at least that it became subsumed into a massive investigation of the cosmos and humanity's place within it. In the context of his sense of a profound planetary emergency – what would now be described as an ecological crisis – Reich developed more and more heroic and confrontational forms of clinical practice, aiming to work always faster and more drastically, to "smash" the armouring of individuals so they could join the project of liberation. Ultimately, he lost faith in the possibility of "straightening the bent tree" of the adult bodymind, and concluded that the only effective approach was to change how children were raised.

Some of Reich's work on character, resistance, and clinical technique has been subsumed into psychoanalysis; but he has also become a major influence on humanistic psychology and the human potential movement. This happened largely through the mediation of Alexander Lowen and bioenergetics (1975), and to a lesser extent through other figures such as Charles Kelley (1974) and David Boadella (1987). It has been a two-way process of influence, with Reich's body-centredness and positive valuation of sexuality (unfortunately only *hetero*sexuality – see below) influencing humanistic therapy, and the latter's optimistic positivism and anti-intellectual slant also colouring many forms of neo-Reichian work.

The assimilation of Reich into the humanistic growth movement went rather against the tenor of his own thinking. Any reader will discover that, although an extremely concrete thinker, he was anything but anti-intellectual. And while believing – against the grain of most Freudian thinking – that human beings are at their core loving and creative, he also saw the need to account for what is destructive and deathly in human behaviour. In other words, Reich is a critical thinker in a much deeper sense than many of those he has influenced; his work carries some of the most complex and difficult elements of psychoanalysis, in particular the challenge of understanding what *appears to be* an innate problem of human existence, an avoidance of pleasure and surrender. Reich argues that it is this that produces, as well as repressive and destructive social formations, such bitter resistance to therapeutic change. Humanistic and body-oriented therapy have tended to replace this problem either with a simplistic opposition between individual (good) and society (bad), or with nothing at all.

As I have already suggested, Reich has a thoroughly concrete understanding of Freud's concept of libido or sexual energy, asserting that the blocking of sexual satisfaction creates neurosis. He translates Freud's somewhat vague notion of dammed-up "psychic energy" into a very precise concept of blocked *muscular* energy.

> *All our patients report that they went through periods in childhood in which, by means of certain practices in vegetative behaviour (holding the breath, tensing the abdominal muscular pressure, etc.), they learned to suppress their impulses of hate, anxiety, and love. ... It can be said that* every muscular rigidity contains the history and meaning of its origin.
> (Reich, 1973, p. 300, original emphasis)

Unlike Freud, Reich *speaks from the side of the body*. In Freud's view, mental processes both do and should control bodily ones, deciding whether or not to permit energetic and emotional discharge. For Reich, domination of the body by the mind – through the illusion that the two are separate – is the root of neurosis, and the "binding of vegetative energy" must be dissolved through emotional discharge. This discharge is not a *result* of the recovery of traumatic memory, but its *cause*: "[T]he concentration of a vegetative excitation and its breakthrough reproduce the remembrance" (Reich, 1973, p. 315).

Reich gives concrete meaning to Freud's conceptualisation of the ego as formed through *binding psychic energy*. He anchors bound and unbound energy in the state of the musculature, and hence of the autonomic nervous system (ANS): chronic tension of the voluntary musculature, associated with dominance of the sympathetic branch of the ANS, is the concrete form in which "mind" (ego) seeks to dominate "body" (id), by "tying up" desir-

ing impulses (Reich, 1972, pp. 286–295). He sees
the split between "mind" and "body" as illusory and
alienated, deriving from this state of chronic muscle
tension, which leads to a developing identification
between "spastic ego" and the processes of thinking
– processes that are actually as bodily as digestion (cf.
Totton, 1998, Ch. 7; Winnicott, 1949).

AN EXAMPLE OF REICH'S CLINICAL WORK

Reich's case histories are among the richest and
most useful resources the BP tradition possesses. Here is a summary of one, to illustrate what I
have written above. This case is described at much
greater length in *The Function of the Orgasm* (Reich,
1973, pp. 309–329).

The patient, as one would have called him
then, showed two notable features: an extreme superficiality, politeness, and unaggressiveness, which
Reich describes as his "psychic reserve", and also
a "very striking facial expression" – a small tight
mouth which hardly moved as he talked. During

six and a half months of at least six-a-week sessions (which was how psychoanalysts used to work), Reich encouraged his patient to "give in to every impulse", repeatedly pointing out to him how he held his mouth.

> *Following the consistent description of the rigid attitude of his mouth, a clonic [i.e., jerky] twitching of his lips set in, weak at first but growing gradually stronger. He was surprised by the involuntary nature of this twitching and defended himself against it.*
> (Reich, 1973, p. 311)

Reich encourages the patient to let the twitching happen:

> *His lips began to protrude and retract rhythmically and to hold the protruded position for several seconds … His face took on the unmistakable expression of an*

infant ... [Over time] the various mani-
festations in his face [twisting with sobs
or apparent rage]... gradually aroused the
patient's interest. This must have some spe-
cial meaning, he said.
(Ibid., p. 311)

For a long while the facial expressions, even
when they quite plainly portray grief or anger, are
not accompanied by felt emotion. Reich realises
that the muscle tensions in the face represent:

... not only the warded-off affect [i.e. feeling]
but also the defense ... The smallness and
cramped attitude of his mouth could, of
course, be nothing other than the expression
of its opposite, the protruding, twitching,
crying mouth.
(Ibid., pp. 312–213)

"Several weeks passed" – that is, twenty or
more sessions of patient, repetitive work with the

facial twitch – before the grief and anger began to show themselves more fully, still without emotional involvement, but with the patient having:

> *... an immediate grasp of the meaning of his action, without any explanation on my part. He knew that he was expressing an overwhelming anger which he had kept locked up in himself for decades. The emotional detachment subsided when an attack produced the remembrance of his older brother, who had very much dominated and mistreated him as a child.*
> (Ibid., p. 314)

The work moves flexibly between bodily and verbal channels, as the patient's emotional charge shifts from bodily to mental focus and back again. "It is not customary in character-analytic work to deal with a subject, no matter how topical, unless the patient enters upon it of his own accord in a fully affective way" (ibid., p. 317). The patient speaks with detachment while his body reacts emotionally, so Reich chooses to stay with the body expression until the emotion comes into the words. The spasms and twitchings spread gradually into the chest and belly, and then jump to the legs, with a "very pleasurable" sensation of discharging tension. But there is still no emotional experience even in these dramatic bodily events.

To progress further Reich steps back and considers the client's character.

> *I began to deal with his caution, not from the psychic side, as I am usually in the habit of doing in character analysis, but from the somatic side. For instance, I pointed out again and again that, while it was true he revealed his anger in his muscular actions, he never followed through, never really struck with his raised and clenched fist … After consistently working on the defense against the muscular action for a number of sessions, the following episode from his*

fifth year of life suddenly occurred to him.
(Ibid., p. 319)

The patient describes a betrayal by his mother, connecting it with both "his defensive attitude towards women" and his general character trait of caution. However, the holding-back continues. One day, the patient begins to talk about his enthusiasm for trout fishing, and describes in detail the process of casting the line and so on. "He had an enormously greedy, almost sadistic expression on his face. It struck me that ... he omitted one detail, namely the moment at which the trout bites into the hook" (ibid., p. 320).

It takes another four weeks before a breakthrough happens and the patient's body manifests the fish caught on a hook:

> *Strange twitchings appeared in the abdomen ... The upper part of his body jerked forward, the middle of his abdomen remained still, and the lower part of his*

body jerked towards the upper part. The entire response was an organic unitary movement. There were sessions in which this movement was repeated continuously … In one such attack, his face had the unmistakable expression of a fish. Without any prompting on my part, before I had drawn his attention to it, the patient said "I feel like a primordial animal," and shortly afterward, "I feel like a fish."
(Ibid., p. 320)

Reich says: "His caution became understandable now: he did not trust anyone. He did not want to be caught." And now real change occurs:

In the process of working through this connection, his personality underwent a conspicuous change. His superficiality disappeared; he became serious. The seriousness appeared very suddenly during one of the sessions. The patient said liter-

ally: "I don't understand; everything has become so deadly serious all of a sudden." (Ibid., p. 321)

Through the image emerging from the body, Reich and his patient discover his relationship with the dangerously seductive and untrustworthy mother; as a result, genital sensations of excitement and pleasure which had felt too dangerous to experience began to emerge, together with a new sense of contact with the world. Later in the work, through a similar embodied image of a gorilla, they discover his relationship with the father.

The patient experienced a severe attack of anxiety. He jumped up, his mouth contorted with pain; beads of perspiration covered his forehead; his musculature was stiff as a board. He hallucinated an animal, an ape. In doing so, his hand had the bent attitude of an ape's paw, and he uttered sounds from the depth of his chest, "as if without vocal

chords", he himself said afterward. It was as if someone had come very close to him and threatened him. Then, trance-like, he cried out, "Don't be angry, I only want to suck."
(Ibid., pp. 325–326)

The "fish" betrayed by the mother, the "ape" threatened by the father: once these two primordial figures have emerged from the body armouring, the work can be completed, as the patient realises he believes – his body believes, so to speak – that:

"A man is hard and unyielding; any form of surrender is feminine"... Immediately following this realisation, his infantile conflict with his father was resolved. On the one hand, he felt sheltered and protected by his father ... At the same time, he strove to stand on his own feet and be independent of his father ... When he finally experienced surrender ... he was deeply baffled by it. "I would never have

*thought," he said, "that a man can sur-
render too."*
(Ibid., pp. 327–328)

Although we may not often have the opportunity to work at this depth, I think most body
psychotherapists will recognise the process Reich
describes. The emergence of other-than-human figures and the reconnection with the cosmos are no
accidents, but constant features of both Reich's case
histories and BP in general (Totton, 2015, Ch. 12).

THE REICHIAN TRADITION

Many therapists have followed in Reich's foot-
steps, sometimes taking up the least creative
aspects of his work. Different neo-Reichian
therapies originate in different phases of his life,
beginning with those who were his students in
Norway after he fled Germany in 1934. At this
point Reich described his work as "character-analytic vegetotherapy" ("vegeto-" meaning "growing"

or "alive"). A significant therapeutic tradition emerged through students like Ola Raknes and Nic Hoel, and is still alive today, inspiring significant new submodalities like Bodynamics. A creative connection was made between Reich's work and a lively network of physiotherapists within mental institutions in Scandinavia, leading to the development by Gerda Boyesen of Biodynamic massage and therapy, which has spread around the world.

By the time Reich moved to the USA in 1940, his interest had largely shifted to the study of what he named "orgone energy" and believed to be a universal life force permeating and shaping the cosmos on every level, including within the human body. He now saw armouring as a process that turned orgone against itself and transformed it into a deathly energy. His therapeutic method was renamed "orgonomy", and became more and more strongly confrontational as Reich increasingly felt an urgency to facilitate change.

Reich was prosecuted and imprisoned by

the American authorities for claiming to have invented a cancer cure (he didn't), and imprisoned for contempt of court because he rejected the court's authority over scientific issues. The real point seems to have been his highly positive views around sex. His books were burnt in the USA as they had been by the Nazis; Reich died in prison of a heart attack in 1957.

Orgonomy still exists as a fundamentalist "church of Reich", but a much more influential therapeutic approach was developed by Alexander Lowen, a student of Reich's who called his own work "Bioenergetics", consciously shaping it to be more palatable to the public. Lowen's approach was highly active, including dozens of exercises that people can use for themselves to raise energy and confront their own armouring: an American can-do approach, paralleled by a shift from Reich's focus on surrender in a lying-down position to Lowen's focus on self assertion and standing up. Like many post-Reichian schools, Bioenergetics follows Reich's positivistic tendencies, asserting a specific concept of human health and normality that includes a prescriptive account of sexuality, privileging heterosexual, penetrative intercourse and treating everything else as neurotic: a view perhaps forgivable for Reich in the 1930s (though Freud himself had moved beyond it), but conservative for the 1960s, and absurdly reactionary for the small BP minority who maintain it today.

In the 1960s and 1970s Reich's ideas spread widely through the culture, exerting an important influence on student power movements and yippy radicalism, though often in diluted and simplified forms. His influence has been an element in several modalities, in particular Gestalt therapy where Fritz Perls was directly influenced by Reich, who had been his analyst, and also through a large variety of later neo-Reichian schools: perhaps most significantly the Hakomi Method, which has a strong spiritual flavour; Charles Kelley's Radix; and David Boadella's Biosynthesis.

NON-REICHIAN SOMATIC THERAPIES

While neo-Reichian schools were proliferating, several forms of body-focused therapy with the body emerged that were not primarily Reichian. These include Focusing, Primal therapies, Holotropic Breathwork, and Process-Oriented Psychology, each of which I will now briefly discuss; and also the whole field of dance and movement therapy, which is beyond the range of this book, but nonetheless closely entwined with body psychotherapy. I should also acknowledge the great influence on body psychotherapies of practices like yoga, breathwork, and the various martial arts, along with meditation (which often focuses on breathing) and other spiritual practices.

Focusing was developed by Eugene Gendlin (1926–2017); while not originally a psychotherapy, it has many similarities, and indeed there are now trainings in Focusing-Oriented Therapy. The central technique is to identify a life issue and become aware of a bodily state or experience that accompanies it; then to gently interrogate that "felt sense" until a shift occurs. Some focusers suggest that the felt sense is at the heart of all successful psychotherapy. Although focusing is often perceived as non-relational, Gendlin stated that "the relationship is of first importance, listening comes second, and focusing instructions come only third" (1998, p. 297).

Primal therapies are a sheaf of approaches emphasising regression to early phases of life, often including birth, pre-birth, and even conception; they find very detailed parallels between adult experiences and archaic ones, which are generally only remembered unconsciously until recovered in therapy. A number of people in the US and in Europe work with pre- and perinatal material. Primal approaches go back to Otto Rank, one of Freud's early followers, and seem to be constantly rediscovered; one can make a rough division between approaches like that of Arthur Janov, which emphasise emotional discharge, and those grouped under the name of Primal Integration that seek to weave primal experiences more gently and subtly into the whole fabric of the bodymindspirit.

Holotropic Breathwork was developed by Stanislav and Christina Grof. Stanislav had previously made important contributions to primal integration with his theory of Basic Perinatal Birth Matrices (Grof, 1975); later, the Grofs used continuous deep breathing, together with music and other scene setters, to access emotionally charged memories. There are close parallels between Holotropic Breathwork and Rebirthing, which also uses continuous "circular" breathing accompanied by "affirmations", positive slogans chosen to counteract existing negative scripts that arise from traumas.

Process-Oriented Psychology is not a subset of somatic therapy, but a large and rich therapeutic modality in its own right, which includes body-focused work as an important element but not privileged above other elements. Developed by Arnold Mindell (b. 1940) and now known as processwork, the approach is flexible and playful in style, studying the relationship between "primary process" – aspects of our experience with which we identify – and "secondary process" – aspects that we find it hard to own, but that are trying insistently to enter our awareness via one channel or another. The relationship between the two is in constant flux as we encounter and move through "edges" – thresholds of resistance to out-of-awareness aspects of reality (Mindell, 1985).

Secondary process often manifests in the body as symptoms, unwelcome experiences that feel "foreign" and threatening to us. Processwork encourages the individual to make friends with, relate with, and amplify their symptom, giving it a voice so as to access the positive information that it contains. Embodiment is seen as one channel, alongside many others, in which process can manifest; therapists are trained to follow their client's process as it twists and turns through different channels of experience. Mindell was once a Jungian analyst, and the influence of Jung's thought on his work may be evident even in this very brief account.

THE 1990S "TURN TO THE BODY"

Between the 1970s human potential movement and the 1990s, body psychotherapy was almost entirely out of the centre of psychotherapy, and also quite ghettoised in itself, with little communication either between different schools or between any of them and the therapeutic mainstream. The cultural appetite for growth was large enough that many BP modalities could do quite well and attract a number of clients and trainees; but they were big fish in a relatively small pond, and to a considerable degree stuck in old theories and practices. This situation made them appear rather cult-like from the outside, which for a minority was to some extent accurate.

The biggest single factor in changing this situation was the extraordinary way in which neuroscience research began to confirm BP's central tenets. This included not only the overall belief in the inseparability of body and mind (Damasio, 1994, 2000), but many quite detailed positions –

for example the embodied nature of trauma, the body's capacity to store unconscious memories and "keep the score" (Van der Kolk, 2014), and the reparative effect of consciously experiencing historic bodily affect in conditions of safety and support. These sensational findings led many therapists to become interested in body psychotherapy, which experienced a startling change in status.

Other important factors synchronised with this: on the one hand the general "turn to the body" that has reached into social and cultural studies, philosophical and political thought, and cognitive research; and, on the other hand, the sudden urgency to "professionalise" that hit the therapy world at much the same time. Therapy had been a largely unregulated and surveillance-free "liberated zone" where people could quietly get on with their work; when this began to change, body psychotherapy responded both institutionally and conceptually, as a whole flock of up-and-coming practitioners decided that BP needed a full upgrade of its theory and practice. In the UK, the Chiron Centre played a very important role in this (Hartley, 2009). In the next chapter we will look at the effects and ongoing progress of that upgrade.

SUGGESTED READING

Grossinger, R. (1995). *Planet Medicine*. 2 vols. Berkeley, CA: North Atlantic.

Heller, M. C. (2012). *Body Psychotherapy: History, Concept, Methods*. New York: W. W. Norton.

Reich, W. (1973). *The Function of the Orgasm*. New York: Farrar, Straus & Giroux. First published in English in 1942. Tr. Vincent R Carfagno.

Sharaf, M. (1984). *Fury on Earth: A Biography of Wilhelm Reich*. London: Hutchinson.

Totton, N. (1998). *The Water in the Glass: Body and Mind in Psychoanalysis*. London: Rebus Press/Karnac.

Totton, N. (2003). *Body Psychotherapy: An Introduction*. Maidenhead, UK: Open University Press.

Young, C. (Ed.) (2011). *The Historical Basis of Body Psychotherapy*. Stow, Galashiels, UK: Body Psychotherapy Publications.

$$\text{\large 2}$$

"BODY PSYCHOTHERAPY 2.0"

The effect of the shift described at the end of the last chapter was that in the 1990s body psychotherapy moved out of its bunker and began to communicate with the rest of the world. This enabled it to challenge and enrich a psychotherapy community that had generally drifted too far away from embodiment; and equally, challenged BP to measure itself against what other modalities and organisations were doing and to identify some serious gaps in its own procedures and understandings.

Paradoxically, therefore, the "turn to the body" in verbal psychotherapy was mirrored by a "turn to the mind" in body psychotherapy, as it caught up with what had been going on for the last half century or so. Temporarily, it was perhaps in danger of losing sight of its central theme of embodiment, and becoming just another variant of talking therapy. But this *was* only temporary, and BP ended up deeper and wider to the extent that it could now reasonably claim to be a more inclusive and holistic approach than talking therapy.

In this chapter I will describe the new version of body psychotherapy, and the dialogues in which it originated: with other therapeutic modalities, especially psychoanalysis, but also with the whole range of current understandings about the bodymind – in particular neuroscience and infant development, but also complexity theory, phenomenology, cognitive science, social theory, and other disciplines. I will begin by discussing the creative engagement between BP and relational psychoanalysis.

THE EMBODIED RELATIONAL TURN

Relational psychoanalysis has only fairly recently emerged as a separate submodality, first in the USA and then worldwide. Originating in a synthesis created by Stephen Mitchell and others (Greenberg & Mitchell, 1983; Mitchell, 2000), it emphasises the crucial role of the relationship between client and therapist, adopting, in place of the traditional "one-person model" where all the attention was focused on the client's material and the therapist was cast as an objective observer, a "two- person model" that treats both participants as emotionally invested and fallible human beings.

It is perhaps not irrelevant that these two perspectives have traditionally been referred to as "one- and two-*body*" models (Balint, 1950); and relational analysis has made strong connections with embodiment-oriented approaches, in particular through the Boston Change Process Study Group's (2010) use of theories of embodied knowledge to develop a concept of "implicit relational knowing": "the domain of knowing how to do things with others", a knowledge that is "as much affective and interactive as cognitive" and that, like knowing how to ride a bicycle or indeed how to walk, "may never become symbolically coded" but "typically operates outside focal attention and conscious experience, without benefit of translation into language" (BCPSG, 2010, p. 31).

Having originally defined itself through re-jecting Freudian drive theory, relational analysis has come back to the body by a different route (Aron, 1998). The BCPSG firmly established that our knowledge about relating is embodied; and re-lational analysts have explored this link from many directions, leading to the slowly dawning realisa-tion of the need to go beyond abstract one-person formulations like "embodied countertransference" to something much more mutual – that the thera-py room is a meeting place not only of two minds, but of two *bodies*, which incorrigibly influence and affect, attract and repel each other.

For almost all analysts, including relational ones, actually working directly with the body has been a bridge too far. (See the fascinating dialogue between body psychotherapist William Cornell and psychoanalyst Sue Shapiro: Cornell, 2009a, 2009b; Shapiro, 2009.) However, the ideas of relational psychoanalysis were communicated to a number of body psychotherapists, particularly in the UK, sparking an enormously fruitful interaction that, after over half a century, reconnected Reichian therapy to its psychoanalytic ancestry, and reminded us just how relational Reich's own approach was: "The *first* impulse of *every* creature must be the desire to establish contact with the outer world" (Reich, 1972, p. 271, original italics). Some important figures in this process were Roz Carroll (2005, 2009, 2014), Shoshi Asheri (2009, 2018), Michael Soth (2005, 2006, 2009), William Cornell (2009a, 2009b, 2015) and myself (Totton, 2003, 2007, 2015).

The core claims of the embodied relational paradigm can be stated as follows:

*Embodiment and relationship are insep-
arable, both in human existence and in
the practice of body psychotherapy. If we
explore embodiment, we encounter relationship; if we explore relationship, we
encounter embodiment. Therapy is more
powerful when the practitioner is able to
recognise the constant interplay between
these two aspects of being human, and to
follow and support the shifts of charge from
one to the other.*
(Totton, 2015, p. xvi)

Hence working with embodiment in therapy
requires therapists to track and consider their own
embodied experience as they sit with the client,
asking themselves how it reflects and descants on
what the client is saying and doing and what the
therapist is thinking and feeling in response. The
emphasis of body psychotherapy conducted in this
way shifts from a *visual* paradigm where the therapist observes the client body and makes deductions

about their process, to a *visceral* paradigm where the client's process directly affects and impacts on the therapist's embodiment.

THE APPLIANCE OF SCIENCE

As stated in the previous chapter, body psychotherapy received an enormous fillip from neuroscience's validation of so many of its core positions. This naturally led some BP practitioners to study neuroscience, including talking with neuroscientists, who were equally intrigued to find that a form of psychotherapy had been working the same territory. This interchange has led to some interesting hybridisation, creating new submodalities where neuroscience actually leads and shapes their approach to embodiment. A good example is Sensorimotor Psychotherapy (Ogden, Minton, & Paine, 2006), which draws very heavily on neuroscientific ideas as frameworks for trauma-based therapy.

More commonly, body psychotherapy has adopted a leavening of neuroscientific concepts to enrich and support insights it already possesses. Roz Carroll writes:

> *By providing a description of human processes from a different perspective, [neuroscience] offers us feedback for us to chew over. ... I believe that neuroscience can be on our side in the argument that people need people, that psychotherapy needs due time for its process, and that simple statistical facts cannot adequately present complex effects of psychotherapy.*
> (Carroll, 2012, p. 23)

The relationship with neuroscience (and also with psychoanalysis) has, I think, combined with a general trend towards "professionalisation" to encourage greater caution and precision in body psychotherapy, an awareness of the risks of retraumatising clients through overly gung-ho methods. This is certainly no bad thing: BP 1.0 had a tendency to rely on personal charisma and good intentions, sometimes at the expense of common sense and thoughtfulness. Once the excitement faded, however, there was not a great deal of neuroscience that seemed to definitely offer BP something new.

One exception was Stephen Porges's Polyvagal Theory, positing the Social Engagement System or SES (Porges, 2011, Porges & Dana, 2018), a new interpretation of the autonomic nervous system (see Chapter 3) focusing on one part of its parasympathetic side. A crude summary of a complex picture would be that the parasympathetic is about calming and smoothing and relaxing, while the sympathetic side is about activating and waking up. The vagal nerve is a large cranial nerve forming a major part of the parasympathetic system, running from the skull right down through the torso.

Porges studied one vagal branch that works to calm and relax the heart (the other branch functions similarly with the guts), and shows that it offers a titratable way to rapidly stimulate the heart and the metabolism in general, by *lessening* its action: if the vagal nerve is *less* activated, the heart will be *more* activated – a much more flexible and less earth-shaking alternative to the sympathetic system's adrenalin-based stimulation, one that can be easily ramped up and down without leaving us exhausted.

The vagal nerve energises us to act in the world without employing fight–flight–freeze ways of processing. It is a precise tool for social interaction, offering exactly the appropriate level of activation to the situation, smoothly adjustable as the situation changes. Normally, the sympathetic will only get activated if this vagal parasympathetic system is not working properly – like using a sledgehammer to crack a nut because the nutcrackers are broken.

Porges points out that this vagal branch is one of several cranial nerves from the same brain region that, in our early aquatic ancestors, regulated the function of the gills. Some are still concerned with breath, and also with sucking, swallowing, salivation, and vocalisation – all the mechanisms that enable breastfeeding without suffocation, and eventually articulate speech. Others let us tense the muscles of the middle ear, and thus pick out speech frequencies from background noise. Others control the expressive muscles of the face, also eyelid muscles, influencing eye contact. All in all, an elaborate and subtle system for human interrelating, as infants and then as adults, developed over evolutionary time by co-opting and synthesising pre-existing features.

Porges describes a complex interactive network of cranial nerves and functional systems originally concerned with absorbing oxygen from water; gradually developing in mammals into a system for absorbing food and comfort from the mother's breast; and then in humans combined with visual and vocal interaction with carers, becoming in adults a system for absorbing *relational* nourishment from our social context. The whole SES is focused on the heart, on the ability of good nourishing relating to calm and soften the heart: it offers neuroscientific backing for the experience of *heart-to-heart contact*. As we shall see in Chapter 3, it also fleshes out and makes concrete the body psychotherapy concept of facing.

Porges's theory says that we are born ready to go, socially speaking: our social, relational energy is *bodily* energy, which needs to be plugged into a live relationship in order to develop. If this doesn't happen successfully, either for internal reasons or because our carers fail to meet us in the dance of social engagement, the body falls back on cruder, earlier, less subtly adjustable systems of activation, the sympathetic nervous system's fight–flight or the parasympathetic strategy of freezing and dissociation.

An important aspect of the Social Engagement System theory is its focus on the biological conditions that allow human social bonding. As Porges says, drawing on the work of his partner Sue Carter (e.g., 2005):

> *Social behaviors associated with nursing, reproduction, and the formation of strong pair bonds require a unique biobehavioral state characterized by immobilization without fear, and immobilization without*

*fear is mediated by a co-opting of the neural
circuit regulating defensive freezing behav-
iors through the involvement of oxytocin.*
(Porges, 2005, p. 33)

Again, Porges is discussing an evolutionary
repurposing (known as "exaptation"): a parasympathetic system for defensive freezing has
developed into a way to relax and stay in contact
even under strong stimulus – something of obvious
relevance to psychotherapy. An attractive feature
of polyvagal theory is that it represents a progres-
sion from the attachment model, with its focus on
mother–infant relationships, to a theory of *social
bonding*, of adult–adult relationship, which builds
on infant attachment but transforms it into peer
interaction.

Porges's work is a scientific theory that actually illuminates and carries forward elements of body
psychotherapy. A further significant input comes
from complexity theory, the study of non-linear
dynamic systems (NDS), which include all living

systems, humans and human relationships among them. In an NDS, change happens not only gradually and incrementally but also through sudden shifts into "self-organisation". Non-linear systems are never static, but in constant flux to one degree or another; and when the system moves sufficiently far from equilibrium and towards "the edge of chaos" (Kauffman, 1995), a very small change of conditions can flip it from one stable state into a different one – a liquid suddenly freezing when it becomes only very slightly colder, or turning to gas when it becomes slightly warmer.

This flip between states is a powerful way of thinking about therapeutic change. Mathematically, it can be described as shifting from a "periodic attractor" – a place in psychological or other space to which we return repeatedly – to a "strange attractor", which emerges at the edge of chaos to shift us into new and unexpected places; in particular, out of the "stuckness" that can result from trauma. The energy for a shift to the edge of chaos often emerges from the *structural coupling* of client and therapist, their organisms coming into entrained synchrony, so that a new and unpredictable system is created (Totton, 2015, pp. 161–166).

INFANT DEVELOPMENT

A parallel to this structural coupling is also at the heart of the infant development research that has had a deep influence on body psychotherapy. The work of Daniel Stern, Colwyn Trevarthen, and others has illuminated the extent to which babies, rather than being the passive recipients of care and attention that was the traditional model, are born actively seeking and initiating relationship, a primary way in which they learn about the world and how to act in it.

Perhaps every generation theorises babies to reflect its own issues; and certainly the revolution in infant development studies, as soon as it was presented, immediately appeared obvious – because relationality is such a current theme. Extending Winnicott's radical concept of the mother–baby dyad, this new paradigm presents a baby who is in many ways an equal participant in forming the dyad through matching and mirroring the carer's vocal and facial signals and rhythmically attuning to their behaviour (Stern, 1985; Trevarthen & Aitken, 2001). Exploring these interactions led Stern to introduce the concept of "vitality affect", dynamic styles that operate transmodally across different expressive channels like movement and voice – naming in a clear way something that can be retrospectively seen as crucial to Reich's work (see Chapter 1).

Daniel Stern was a member of the Boston Change Process Study Group mentioned earlier – a direct link between the study of relationality in infant care dyads and in therapy. Both these areas clearly connect with neuroscience and the concepts of self-soothing and self-regulation as capacities we internalise and develop through relationship (Carroll, 2012).

THE "HUMAN SCIENCES"

Just as important a factor as the impacts of relational psychoanalysis, neuroscience and infant development studies was the "turn to the body" in philosophy and social science. This has been a gradual revolution, with some of its roots in the phenomenology of Maurice Merleau-Ponty in the 1950s and early 1960s. Merleau-Ponty only gradually became well known outside France, but his influence has snowballed. He believes that if we examine our experience closely, we find we have direct, unmediated knowledge of the world and other people through what he calls "the Flesh". Merleau-Ponty, and later James and Eleanor Gibson, stress that we grasp cognitively those elements of our environment *with which we have embodied interaction in order to do things*. We could think of it as "just-in-time" perception, analogous with the way supermarkets stock up their branches with the products that are about to run out: organisms perceive those parts of the world, and only those parts of the world, that are immediately needed.

I barely have room here even to make these concepts comprehensible, let alone do them justice. The essential point is that they turned our attention from the idea of *cognition as observation followed by internal modelling* to a reconceptualising of *cognition as an immediate embodied engagement*. This provides theoretical backing for the relational approach that I described earlier, which I called "the shift from the visual to the visceral". More recently, such thinking has seeded a whole school of "embodied cognition" which has become very influential over a number of fields (see *Suggested Reading* below).

In parallel with these developments another French thinker, Michel Foucault, spearheaded a further "turn to the body" in the fields of politics, history, and social science. Foucault drew attention to how various political and social projects can be seen as efforts to discipline and regulate bodies, while simultaneously individuals and groups spend enormous time on "technologies of the self" which attempt to improve and refine our bodies and minds through activities like yoga, gym training, dieting, or, indeed, body psychotherapy. He treats the body as a crucial site of conflict between various forms of power and resistance to power – like a contested territory, repeatedly fought over by outside forces and local guerrillas.

For Foucault, bodies are "produced by discourse"; by this he means that there is no absolute, essential body, but rather numerous ways of describing and experiencing bodies, all of which have political implications. This explodes BP 1.0's fundamentalist account of "*The* Body", and helps to prise open a space for a far richer picture of *many* bodies, with different genders, sexualities, skin colours, kinds and degrees of abledness, all interacting in complex and politically inflected ways. Foucault's work has been taken up and developed further by many feminist and queer theorists (e.g., Budgeon, 2003; Fischer & Dolezal, 2018; Fournier, 2002; Huffer, 2010).

The human sciences turn to the body that I have just sketched has had far less attention from body psychotherapists than either neuroscience or relationality. However, I suggest that the three are imbricated with each other, so that each means far more when taken together and in dialogue with the other two. In particular, neuroscience on its own can be quite negative in its effects on BP, encouraging people to talk and think less about the body and more about the brain, and even about specific sites in the brain that, in phrenological style, are supposed to be the precise location of particular psychological faculties. As Roz Carroll has pointed out in homage to Winnicott's idea that there is no infant without a mother, there is no brain without a body: every brain needs a body, and an environment, to think through and with (cf. Chiel & Beer, 1997).

The cumulative effect of the turns to the body that I have described has been to situate embodiment within a whole universe, with many dimensions including the relational, social, and political, also including – another rich area we cannot explore here – the other-than-human world that we oddly tend to call "nature", as if we were not ourselves natural (Totton, 2011). The overall effect has been to make BP less dogmatic and more tentative in its assumptions about embodiment, and at the same time more able to engage with the real experience of its clients and practitioners.

In the space available I have only been able to give a few important examples of the creative interplay that began in the 1990s between body psychotherapy and the wider world of human thought. This is still very much a work in progress; who knows where it will end. I now turn briefly to the organisational aspects of that interplay.

ORGANISATIONAL DEVELOPMENTS

Just as body psychotherapy has over recent decades started to emerge from its conceptual bunker, so it has started emerging from its institutional bunker. Here it has made enormous strides, forming new institutions of its own and finding new relationships with the institutions of psychotherapy in general. This has obvious great advantages, but perhaps also some downsides.

In 1988 the European Association for Body Psychotherapy was formed. As of 2018, it has over 800 members in around 40 countries (several of them not in Europe), with nine national associations; every two years it puts on a large congress in a different European venue, attended by many more practitioners who are not accredited by EABP. The EABP by no means represents the entire field of BP in Europe – among other reasons, because it is difficult for practitioners in some countries to fulfil its training and practice requirements – but it does form a large segment of the field. In the UK, a 2016 gathering of self-defined body psychotherapists attracted 100 or so people; but there are currently only 26 UK members of EABP. It is impossible to estimate how typical this proportion is. There is currently no global BP organisation, but the EABP fills some of this role, with a scattering of members from many non-European countries; the other significant organisation is the US Association for Body Psychotherapy, with 325 members of whom 18 are in other countries.

The legal situation of psychotherapists, and body psychotherapists in particular, varies a great deal between different countries. Several, including Germany and Italy, require people to qualify as psychologists in order to practise BP. Ironically, this tends to put BP on an equal footing with other psychotherapies – they are all equally restricted! In some other countries, while psychotherapy in general is permitted, BP is not recognised on a par with other modalities. The main purpose of the European Association for Psychotherapy (EAP) is to push for psychotherapy in general to have equal status as a profession alongside psychology and psychiatry, and EABP has put a great deal of effort, with some success, into having BP recognised in the pan-European standards developed by the EAP; among other things this has involved gathering evidence for its scientific validity (see the Research section in Chapter 4).

The fight to gain recognition across Europe has meant that EABP has worked towards a considerable level of standardisation of BP training – a total shift from the old dispensation where different modalities had completely distinct systems, theories, and training methods. To gain EAP recognition, trainings have to conform to a universal model, a master's-level four-year part-time course; there is also strong pressure for integration and common curricula, to the extent that some schools offer a generic training in body psychotherapy. I think there is enough discussion in this book of the diversity within BP to thoroughly problematise the idea of a generic training, which I suggest would mean leaving out entirely a great deal of BP's most creative work. A lot of one thing, a little bit of everything, or a sort of generalised fudge? These are to some degree always the three choices for a psychotherapy training.

Another aspect of organisational reform has been that BP schools and membership bodies, as with other therapies, have needed to develop formal structures of regulation, monitoring, complaints procedures, and so on: all indubitably necessary and desirable, but, some would argue, perhaps too much adopted wholesale from other sorts of professional organisations, and not sufficiently modulated by psychotherapeutic ways of understanding people and groups.

At the same time that BP has been regularising and unifying itself on an organisational level, a large number of bridges have been built between BP and the wider field of psychotherapy and counselling. The bridges have been built from both sides: BP practitioners have ventured into therapy forums as speakers, writers, and conference attendees, and have invited talking therapists and others to present at BP events, while there has been considerable interest among verbally oriented therapists in adding at least a little experience of somatically oriented ways of working to their toolkit. Speaking for myself, as a well-established BP practitioner I have found my available time for leading workshops fairly evenly divided between training students of body psychotherapy, and offering a variety of talks, seminars, and workshops to students and practitioners across the whole field of psychotherapy. Many of my clients have always been more or less unaware that I define myself as a body psychotherapist – a lot of them call what we do together "counselling", a term I have never used.

In the UK body psychotherapists have always had the same legal standing as any other practitioners, and some BP trainings are or have been organisational members of the UK Council for Psychotherapy (UKCP) which regulates the field on a voluntary basis (there is still no state regulation of psychotherapy, largely because so many therapists oppose it). Some individual body psychotherapists have achieved very senior positions in UKCP, with one coming close to being elected chair. The Minster Centre, one of the most respected integrative trainings in the UK, has several senior body psychotherapists on its staff, some of them teaching somatically aware relational work rather than specifically BP. These are examples of how far BP has come towards mainstream acceptance.

SUGGESTED READING

Anderson, F. S. (2008). *Bodies in Treatment: The Unspoken Dimension*. New York: Analytic Press.

Aron, L., & Anderson, F. S. (Eds.) (1998). *Relational Perspectives on the Body*. London: Routledge, 2009.

Dana, D. (2018). *The Polyvagal Theory in Therapy: Engaging the Rhythm of Regulation*. New York: W. W. Norton.

Fogel, A. (2013). *Body Sense: The Science and Practice of Embodied Self-Awareness*. New York: W. W. Norton.

Stern, D. N. (1985). *The Interpersonal World of the Infant*. New York: Basic Books.

Thompson, E. (2007). *Mind in Life.* Cambridge, MA: Harvard University Press.

Totton, N. (2015). *Embodied Relating: The Ground*

of Psychotherapy. London: Karnac/Routledge.

Varela, F. J., Thompson, E., & Rosch, E. (1991). *The Embodied Mind: Cognitive Science and Human Experience.* Cambridge, MA: MIT Press.

White, K. (Ed.) (2014). *Talking Bodies: How Do We Integrate Working with the Body in Psychotherapy from an Attachment and Relational Perspective?* London: Karnac/Routledge.

CONCEPTS, TECHNIQUES, RESEARCH

In this chapter I will try to give a sense of what body psychotherapists do, and why they do it – the practice, and the thinking behind it. Some of this may feel quite exotic and hard to grasp; but the reality is that quite a lot of BP practitioners' time is spent apparently doing the same thing that people expect all psychotherapists to do – sitting and listening. What is going on *inside* the therapist, however, may be rather different.

THE THINKING BEHIND BODY PSYCHOTHERAPY

Bodymind and embodiment

Body psychotherapy treats each human being as essentially a unity, existing simultaneously and entirely in both the realm of embodiment and the realm of mentality: hence, a "bodymind". This is not as mystical as it may sound – to be simultaneously an embodied mind and a self-aware body is an entirely ordinary experience, but our language is not well-equipped to discuss it. Some body therapists would extend this to a third realm and speak of "bodymindspirit". The implication is that an individual can be approached and accessed equally from any of these viewpoints, body, mind, and/or spirit, whichever is most accessible at a given moment.

"Embodiment" refers both to the ordinary state of being a bodymind, and also to the less ordinary state of consciously *experiencing* this. Conger (1994, p. 195) describes embodiment, simply but resonantly, as "being at home in your body" – rather than alienated from it, feeling like a mind facilitated, obstructed, or even attacked by "its" body. The body psychotherapist uses her own "at-homeness" as a tool to help the client discover theirs. Of course, my home may have a leaky roof, or even burn down; but it is still my home.

Functional identity
Our nature as united bodymind exemplifies Reich's theory of "orgonomic functionalism", the "functional identity" of psychological and physiological processes:

> *It would be wrong to speak of the "transfer" of physiological concepts to the psychic sphere, for what we have in mind is not an analogy but a real identity: the unity of psychic and somatic function.*
> (Reich, 1972, p. 340)

As well as underlying the concept of bodymind, we shall see this has specific application to several other body psychotherapy concepts.

Charge and energy

Most forms of BP use the term "energy", but it can mean several different things. Freud saw our sexual drive, "libido", as a sort of life energy. Reich understood libido very literally; he explored human bio-electricity, and eventually believed he had discovered a biophysical energy pervading the universe which he called orgone, determining not only our body state, but also weather phenomena and even the formation of galaxies. He made devices called "orgone accumulators" to concentrate this energy, and many people (including me) have had to acknowledge that they can sense something powerful when using them.

Later body psychotherapists responded to this in different ways. For example, Radix substituted for the biophysical concept of orgone the vision of a:

> ... *substratum from which energy and feeling are created and which forms the connecting link between the two ... the si-*

multaneous root of subjective experience
and of bodily expression and movement.
(Kelley, 1974, p. vii)

Moving in the opposite direction, Alexander Lowen writes as if "bioenergy" – a term that he prefers to orgone – is much the same thing as straightforward metabolic energy.

Recent body psychotherapists tend to treat "energy" rather loosely and vaguely, although it is often quite central to their practice. Practitioners decide how to work by assessing the state of the client's *energy*, and perceived changes in body *energy* gives them feedback on the effect of their interventions; many practitioners have a very vivid and detailed experience of *energetic* shifts in their clients. Most other people find this hard to understand – physical scientists would certainly feel the word was being used very unclearly. How metaphorical or how literal is this sort of talk?

"Energy" probably often refers to emotional tone, which many people can assess very sensitively from someone's posture and movement – what Daniel Stern calls "vitality affect" (see below). Sometimes, though, it means something equivalent to an aura, or the Chinese *chi*, or Indian *prana*. All these concepts, although very broadly parallel, cannot be loosely combined: they have distinct and specific qualities. One cannot do acupuncture with orgone, or Reichian therapy with *prana*.

Perhaps most BP practitioners would agree on Richard Strozzi Heckler's formulation:

> *Our energy is our aliveness. It is the stuff that creates the continuity of our life. We wake up with it, we go to bed with it, it is present in our waking and sleeping dreams. … It is the ground from which our living emerges. … In a way energy is nothing special, but it is the glue that binds everything together and connects us to our essential self.* (1984, pp. 58–59)

Vitality affect

This is Daniel Stern's term for dynamic emotional qualities expressed in a range of modalities including movement and voice (Stern, 1985). They define important characteristics of each individual, and BP practitioners need to be able to perceive, discriminate, and have some sort of way to name them. By their very nature, this language is likely to be highly metaphorical. One can often see Reich attempting to describe what we would now call vitality affect, for example in this passage:

> *Others frequently ward off their repressed aggression by "insinuating" – as one such patient once put it – themselves into the favour of any person capable of rousing their aggression. They become as "slippery" as eels, evade every straightforward reaction, can never be held fast. Usually, this "slipperiness" is also expressed in the intonation of their voice; they speak in a soft, modulated, cautious, and flattering way ...*

*the ego itself becomes "greasy" and "slimy"
and conceives of itself in this way.*
(1972, p. 175)

Armouring

As mentioned in Chapter 2, Reich coined this term
for systematic patterns of chronic muscular rigidity that, like armour, are hard, tough, restrictive,
and protective. We develop armouring in response
to chronic trauma – generally the traumas of socialisation rather than any more dramatic events
– through repeatedly inhibiting our impulses for
emotional expression: holding back crying, anger,
etc. sets up muscular armouring. For Reich, armouring begins with holding our breath to repress
feeling, and spreads out from there. Armouring
both embodies repression, and preserves the
"locked-in" repressed impulse. *Muscular* armouring
is functionally identical with *character* armouring
(see below). This was one of the ways in which
Reich realised that body and mind are one.

Some recent neo-Reichian schools see the

role of flaccid, inactive muscles as equally important to rigid ones. Starting out from the work
of Lillemor Johnsen, Bodynamics (Marcher &
Fich, 2010) has developed a systematic study of
how patterns of rigid and flaccid muscles spell
out someone's character structure.

Character
In the Reichian tradition, a person's character
structure is the ensemble of their various armour-
ings, the complex chord created by all the various
notes sounded in their history. Character armour
is the chronic effect of traumatic crises: character
traits embody both the original desire of the child,
and its repression through fear of outside reaction.
"A person's character conserves and at the same
time wards off the function of certain childhood
situations" (Reich, 1973, p. 305). To set character
in stone, so to speak, armouring in a particular area
of the body needs to occur during the appropriate developmental window for that area – tying
together space and time; for example, armouring

around the eyes only sets up what is often called the "schizoid" character if it happens during very early infancy, although later on it will still have an impact on the person.

Reich and many of his successors saw character as primarily pathological, emphasising the systematic patterns of chronic psychological rigidity described in the previous paragraph, and naming them accordingly. More recently, there has been increasing recognition that character *armouring* is not the whole of character. In order to be *here*, we have to be *someone*: that is, we have to take a particular shape, both physically and psychologically – to be more drawn in some directions than in others, displaying some traits more than others.

This in a nutshell is what "character" means: the particular *way in which* we manifest as embodied beings, which expresses as *the way in which* we hold ourselves, talk, move, interact – the vitality affects we display. We can also think of it as a *theme* we follow as we move through life, a motif of existence that stands out for us more than others. If "a person's character is the functional sum total of all past experiences" (Reich, 1973, p. 145), then it embodies all our joys and triumphs as well as all our suffering.

Hence, character can be entirely *creative* in nature – we can be very beautifully and admirably the particular kind of person that we are, following the particular theme that we follow; and some modern character theorists criticise treating it as pathology, and have renamed the positions in less judgemental terms. However, we can get stuck in a groove, fixated exclusively on one particular aspect of life, trying to open every door we encounter with the same key – or perhaps, if our early experience has been very unlucky, with a bit of broken metal we *think* is a key. Character can be a channel for energy, or a block on it. Usually, it has some of each quality.

Our character has four aspects that vary in synchronisation with each other:

- Our developmental history

- Our style of embodiment
- Our core belief system
- Our response – combining resistance and submission – to the ensemble of power relations into which we are born, on both a personal (family) and a social level.

These four aspects of our selves are *functionally identical*, as Reich would say, four ways of describing the same thing. It is through our developmental experience that our style of embodiment and our core beliefs constellate; while our embodiment can be seen as a direct expression of our core beliefs (e.g., "Relaxing equals collapsing", "I must hold in my emotions"). And all three of these aspects – development, embodiment, and beliefs – can be framed as responses to power relations.

Reichian character theory is both powerful and illuminating; it offers a model of individual difference that is historically, somatically, and politically inflected. However, it has tended to be downplayed in many recent versions of body psychotherapy. This seems to result from a humanistic unease about "pigeonholing" people. Certainly character theory can be misused if it is adapted to a medicalised approach of diagnosis and treatment. But the theory itself is precisely a subtle account of *individuality in relationship*, and the strategies and defences used to preserve individual freedom – and the price paid in doing so.

Complexity theory, which I briefly discussed in Chapter 2, offers a dynamic way of thinking about character that helps us understand its stubborn resistance to change (Piers, 2000). A character position cycles around a periodic attractor, like a body in orbit around a planet. It takes a great deal of energy – often provided by a structural coupling with a therapist or another important figure – to shift out of the gravity well and towards a strange attractor that sparks unpredictable change.

Grounding, skying, centring, facing

These orientations can be used as the basis for an alternative way of thinking about human variation, or they can be used in combination with character theory. The idea of a centre or core is another example of functional identity, referring both to the centre of the *self* and the centre of the *body*: "a bodily and energetic base camp" (Heckler, 1984, p. 79), from which energy expands outward into the rest of the body.

This centre is generally understood to be in the viscera and the nerve plexi of the guts; as the least armoured part of the system, contact with it is essential for wellbeing. It also has a spiritual quality, a person's "essential nature" that "does not need fixing" (Conger, 1994, p. 46). The therapeutic work of *centring* is about re-establishing balance between the two halves of the autonomic nervous system, the activating sympathetic and the relaxing parasympathetic side (see below): coming to what craniosacral therapists call a "still-point". Like all these qualities, it is important for practitioners as well as clients: we need to focus inward and find our own core in order to reach outward to the client.

As important as centring, and with a similar functional identity of somatic and psychological meanings, is *grounding*. On one level this refers to a relaxed, responsive state of the leg and pelvis musculature, and a corresponding postural aliveness – only attainable if we have worked through traumatic aspects of the infant experience of learning to stand unsupported. On another level, "by channeling our energetic and bodily experience through our legs and into the earth, we become grounded in the living reality of our situation" (Heckler, 1984, p. 86); so that "not to know how one stands is equivalent to not knowing where one stands or to have no standing as a person" (Lowen, 1976b, pp. 185–186). Hence grounding can become a symbol of the whole state of embodiment.

There is an important distinction between *vertical* and *horizontal* grounding (Southgate,

1980). While Lowen, who introduced the term "grounding", focuses on upright posture and the leg–foot–ground relationship as a basis for active involvement with the world, Reich's earlier work facilitates the equally crucial ability to ground horizontally, lying back and accepting the support of the earth – by extension, grounding our conscious identity in our unconscious and involuntary self. At different moments and for different people, either or both of these can be the important challenge. Grounding through our sitting bones perhaps has some of both qualities.

Em Edmondson and I (Totton & Edmondson, 2009) have suggested the equally significant function of *skying*: the capacity to contact cosmic, visionary, dreaming energies accessed through the crown of our head. Unless we are grounded, this contact will be profoundly destabilising; but similarly, without the sky connection, grounding will tend to become *over*grounding, a heavy, stodgy practicality. Like a tree, human beings function best with their roots in the ground and their branches reaching for the heavens.

David Boadella's biosynthesis works with the three interlinked functions of centring, grounding, and *facing*.

> *Facing … is about having adequate contact with internal and external reality. This includes all our "channels of contact" … especially the eyes and voice.*
> (Labworth & Wilson, 2000, p. 16)

Thus, facing anticipates Porges's Social Engagement System theory (see Chapter 2). Boadella (1987, p. 16) suggests that working with facing is about finding a balance between over-sensitivity and under-sensitivity.

Autonomic nervous system

Reich was ahead of his time in focusing on the autonomic (or "vegetative") nervous system (ANS), which normally functions outside conscious awareness and control, regulating heartbeat, viscera, breathing, and so on. Conventionally, it is opposed to the central nervous system (CNS), which includes the brain and the nerves controlling voluntary movement; but from a more contemporary viewpoint, the ANS is not functionally separate from the CNS, but in close dialogue with it.

Affect, in particular, just as it philosophically unites mind and body (a "feeling" is both a mental and a physical event), neurologically unites the CNS and ANS:

> *Emotion depends on the communication between the autonomic nervous system and the brain; visceral afferents convey information on physiological state to the brain and are critical to the sensory or psychological experience of emotion, and cranial nerves and the sympathetic nervous system are outputs from the brain that provide somatomotor and visceromotor control of the expression of emotion.*
> (Porges, 2011, p. 155)

The Polyvagal Theory links the evolution of the ANS to emotional experience and expression, facial gestures, vocal communication, and associated social behaviour. Porges suggests that the autonomic nervous system can best be thought of as consisting not of two divisions, as traditionally, but three: as well as the sympathetic (alertness, fight–flight) and parasympathetic (relaxation, immobilization), there is the "social engagement system" involved with communication. (See the discussion in Chapter 2.)

Lowen and other neo-Reichians moved from Reich's emphasis on the viscera and autonomic system to an interest in the central nervous system: a shift from unconscious and spontaneous embodiment to conscious control which in many ways parallels the development of psychoanalysis. Perhaps it is very hard for us to stay with and accept the aspects of our being that we cannot control; but body psychotherapy has, or should have, a strong interest in fostering this acceptance.

Self-regulation and trauma
It is through the ANS that we achieve a state of unconscious self-regulation, something that was central for Reich and has been increasingly emphasised by developmental and neuroscientific research.

> *The prototype and initial bridging concept between biology and psychology was self-regulation, modelled on physiological homeostasis and incorporating the behavioural concept of adaptation. ... Mother and baby can be conceived of as homeostatic regulators of each other's emotional states. The baby's behaviour is feedback – a communication to the mother. Her attuned response acts as benign feedback, helping to maintain equilibrium in the infant.*
> (Carroll, 2012, p. 9)

The generally agreed picture is that through this attuned relationship, the infant gradually achieves the ability to self-regulate with increasing robustness, returning to a stable state from the buffetings of life (Schore, 1994). Traumatic events can damage this resilience and reduce or eliminate the ability to self-regulate. Hence the core of contemporary approaches to trauma and PTSD, in body psychotherapy and elsewhere, is to endeavour by one means or another to restore the capacity to self-regulate. This can be done by focusing on safety, self-soothing, and relaxation, or on discharge of shock and other painful emotions (see Introduction, the Trauma/Discharge model), or a combination of both.

Reich's original concept of self-regulation, while consistent with the above, had a somewhat different emphasis on freedom and spontaneity of the personality:

> *Self-regulation follows the natural laws of pleasure and is not only compatible with natural instincts; it is, in fact, functionally identical with them. ... Steadily alternat-*

ing between tension and relaxation, it is consistent with all natural functions. … The person with a healthy, self-regulated structure does not adapt himself to the irrational part of the world; he insists on the fulfilment of his natural rights.
(Reich, 1973, pp. 181–182)

Contrariwise, someone able to live a self-regulated life without interference from others is more likely to be able to sustain somatic self-regulation:

The most important condition for enabling the child to keep its free biological pulsation is self-regulation and the opportunity for alive contact with other people who are themselves tolerably free from anxiety and inhibitions.
(Raknes, 1971, p. 171)

Birth

The primary, universal trauma of human life, according to a number of body psychotherapists, is birth.

> *Birth is a formative drama which can potentiate some of our deepest personality patterns. … Any understanding of later character dynamics rests on this first engagement with the outside world.*
> (Boadella, 1987, p. 38)

Many practitioners, as they work with their clients, are holding the image of birth somewhere in the back of their minds; and this template will be foregrounded if the client, for example, talks about feeling "under pressure" or "squeezed", mentions "light at the end of the tunnel", or produces bodily symptoms like a pressure headache or emotional symptoms like premonitions of disaster. A range of different methods for "birthing" or "rebirthing" have been developed; some

BP practitioners specialise in this area, and many others include it in their bag of resources.

Implicit knowledge, body memory
An important and originally controversial tenet of body psychotherapy is that the body can hold memories that do not exist in the conscious mind, but can be accessed through bodywork. Hence Reich asserts that *"[E]very muscular rigidity contains the history and meaning of its origin"* (Reich, 1973, p. 300, original italics); he describes many situations where the breakthrough of muscular impulse in body therapy is accompanied by both feelings and memories from the early life situation that created the original muscular block. Jack Rosenberg and Marjorie Rand distinguish this from ordinary remembering:

> *Unlike remembering ... it is a profound body mind experience involving all the senses – sight, hearing, smell, taste, touch. Simply remembering doesn't reach most*

*of our early experiences because we had
them before we had language. We retain
the feelings in our bodies ...*
(Rosenberg & Rand, 1985, p. 28)

There is now overwhelming research support
for these ideas, particularly as regards traumatic
experiences; and also some theories of how the
body *can* remember, especially emotional memory (Fogel, 2013, pp. 251–268; Van der Kolk, 2014).

KEY TECHNIQUES OF BODY PSYCHOTHERAPY

Contact

For body psychotherapists, contact is an essential
prerequisite of the work, and also a quality that
the work strives continuously to deepen. Again,
the term is a metaphor derived from bodily experience: it describes the state of being "in touch",
with oneself, with the world, or with another
person – with each of these tending to induce
the others. Contact is what makes the difference

between touching one's lover or child, and touching the person next to one on a commuter train. It is a condition of living relationship, which, as Gestalt therapy reminds us, depends equally on the ability to create a *boundary* between self and other: "contact is the appreciation of differences" (Fritz Perls, quoted in Heckler, 1984, p. 119).

Armouring and contraction create a state of contactlessness (Reich, 1972, pp. 308ff): the individual may wear a mask of vitality and sociality, but is fundamentally out of touch with their own somatic and emotional experience, and similarly out of touch with the world around them and with other people. By sensitively offering the client embodied contact – which may or may not include physical contact – the body psychotherapist seeks to reawaken their ability to feel both self and other. Contact is not just a technical skill, more a way of life:

> *We must first learn how to be with ourselves before we can truly be with others. ...*

*When we are connected with ourself, our
excitement automatically begins to flow
outward, and we weave the fabric of our
lives with the streamings and pulsations of
those around us.*
(Heckler, 1984, p. 122)

Presence
To offer contact effectively, the therapist – or any
person – needs to be fully present to their own
being.

*Contact can take almost any form as long
as we bring an energetic presence to the
form. Contact is how we are with some-
body or something. Presence, which is our
embodied awareness, is the mother of contact. Contact is the process of transmitting
meaningful information ... and it originates
in our living presence.*
(Heckler, 1984, p. 119)

Body psychotherapists also need the ability to recognise the presence or absence of contact, to track it as it waxes and wanes, and to offer it in the form and channel most acceptable to the client, and in a way that is both firm and unthreatening.

Touch
Sometimes contact may be offered through physical touch (see the discussion of issues around this in Chapter 4); and, like a massage therapist, the body psychotherapist needs to have developed a relaxed, warm, confident, reassuring, and gentle touch – hands that are cold and clammy, abrupt, nervous, or invasive will not convey an invitation to contact. This means that the practitioner will need to understand and work through their own issues around touch.

Beyond the basic yet subtle issue of contactful touch, body psychotherapists frequently cultivate what Don Hanlon Johnson (2000) calls "intricate tactile sensitivity" (ITS), using touch to pick up complex information about the immediate and long-term state of their client's embodiment, and also to interact with that state in subtle ways. Johnson identifies three elements that define ITS: first, "*discreteness*", the ability to consciously or preconsciously discriminate different sorts of information, including micro-movements in the client's body, variations in temperature, tissue density and tissue tone, different pulsations, and different reactions to touch. Second, "*pattern sensitivity*", non-verbal perception of movement throughout large segments of the body that can be contacted from touch at one point: the practitioner feels their awareness "reaching out" into the client's body and identifying events which are given names like "blocks", "pulls", "twists", "shears".

The third element he calls "*sensitive contact*" between therapist and client, a unique level or flavour of contact that derives from this deep tactile connection. Many ITS users will certainly recognise this: a profound intimacy stemming from the sense that one is touching the *inside* of a person's body, tracing their bones, cupping their organs, and swaying to the tides of their fluid systems.

Intensive bodywork

Several BP approaches employ hands-on body-work skills that are more interventionist than the techniques mentioned above. For example, some neo-Reichian schools, following Reich's late approach, use deep pressure to force the release of muscle tension and break up restrictions in the connective tissues (Baker, 1967; Painter, 1984). Biodynamic massage (Boyesen, 1980) uses a different set of techniques, some "deep" and some "gentle", towards the same goals. Bioenergetics and some other approaches use exercises and postures to raise energy levels and release blocks (Lowen, 1977).

Breath

Reich pointed out that the fundamental way we stop ourselves *feeling* is to stop ourselves *breathing*.

*Imagine that you have been frightened or
that you anticipate great danger. You will
involuntarily suck in your breath and hold
it. … It is by holding their breath that children are in the habit of fighting against
continual and tormenting conditions of
anxiety … In reduced respiration, less oxygen is introduced … With less energy in
the organism, the vegetative excitations are
less intense and, therefore, easier to control.*
(Reich, 1973, pp. 306–309)

Hence all forms of neo- and post-Reichian
work and many other approaches emphasise restoring the capacity to breathe fully and freely.
Some forcefully "break down" the muscular blocks
against breathing, notably in the diaphragm; others support a sense of safety and relaxation so the
breath will naturally and gradually deepen. It is
not about willed, deliberate deep-breathing, but
surrender to our spontaneous breath.

The experience of breathing provides the most continuous lived bodily form for the ego's fundamental experience of itself. ... As one patient reported: "When I feel my breathing fully, I feel as though I've come into the clear."
(Eigen, 1993, pp. 44–45)

Because free, full breathing involves surrender, it is deeply bound up with the therapeutic relationship: as with free association in psychoanalysis, the client can only allow themselves to open up this deeply if they trust their therapist equally deeply. Hence focusing on breathing is intimate and stirring for both participants, and brings up powerful material. Another way of thinking about the importance of breath is that it occupies the interface between voluntary and involuntary, CNS and ANS: breathing will always keep happening of its own accord, but as soon as we pay attention to it we can control it consciously – in fact, find it hard to restrain ourselves from doing so. Hence its value as an object of meditation.

Hyperventilation
Breathwork in BP can induce a phenomenon known medically as "hyperventilation": the breath becomes both intense and apparently unstoppable, accompanied by painful cramps in the hands, feet, face, and other areas, and often by considerable anxiety. *Physiologically* speaking, the breather has blown too much carbon dioxide out of the body, temporarily changing the blood and muscle chemistry. *Energetically* speaking, breathing has intensified their blocks against expression.

Some forms of BP and bodywork deliberately induce this state; others accept it as a fairly common effect of breathwork. Empirically, someone hyperventilating can be encouraged and supported to "go through" the experience and find their way to a deep but balanced breath – usually a profoundly rewarding and liberating experience, which often confers a degree of immunity against hyperventilating in future. What helps someone get through is encouragement to use their voice, and to use the cramped muscles to grasp, hit, or kick out. Hyperventilation is certainly a powerful, sometimes frightening, and occasionally dangerous tool, which no one, client or practitioner, should use without deliberate and informed choice. Some body psychotherapists are opposed to its use. Spontaneous hyperventilation can usually be mechanically relieved by breathing into and out of a paper bag, recycling carbon dioxide into the body.

Research
There are very different views within the BP world about the value or otherwise of research as a way of either learning about or validating the work. Some would say that intensive, supervised therapy with individual clients is the best, or even the only, way to learn. Others support something more like a conventional "evidence-based" approach aimed at establishing statistical effectiveness and effica-

cy – both as valid in itself, and as a requirement for BP to be accepted in a wider range of settings, specifically in the NHS.

An in-between position supports the role of scientific research, but objects to the identification of this with randomised controlled trials (RCTs), arguing that such an approach is artificially limited:

> ... *just one – out of several – scientific perspectives ... that is being used ... by external forces and by people outside of the profession of psychotherapy to "manage" certain aspects of health care, or insurance pay-outs, or governmental regulations, or professional political processes.*
> (Young, 2012, p. xi)

After all, we need to consider the question: "Effective for what?" If the goal is to find out whether body psychotherapy helps people get back to work at jobs that don't satisfy them, the answer may well be "no"; but arguably this demonstrates its effectiveness rather than the opposite.

Certainly body psychotherapy is comparatively under-researched in terms of RCTs, which, although touted as the "gold standard", are vastly expensive and arguably inappropriate for psychotherapy. However, BP by no means completely lacks an evidence base: much of it consists of case histories, the historically preferred approach to the study of what works in psychotherapy. (On the usefulness of case histories in psychotherapy research, see Jones, 1993; for a phenomenological research model, see Finlay, 2011; for arguments in favour of the case history in medicine, see Nissen & Wynn, 2014).

There is also a growing body of medical-model style research into the effectiveness and efficacy of BP. The rate of development can be seen by comparing May's (2005) overview with Rohricht's (2009, expanded in 2012) overview: as Rohricht points out, in four years "many more studies have been identified … and there is now a much better evidence base for the efficacy" of body-oriented psychotherapy (Rohricht, 2009, p. 146; 2012, p. 268). This process has presumably continued, although there has been no subsequent overview published so far.

One caveat is that Rohricht's survey, unlike May's, covers body-*oriented* psychotherapy (BOP), a considerably wider field than body psychotherapy proper, which for example includes the comparatively well-researched field of Dance Movement Psychotherapy. In any case, Rohricht's conclusion is positive and important:

> *BOP seems to have generally good effects on subjectively experienced depressive and anxiety symptoms, somatisation and social insecurity. Patients undergoing BOP appear to benefit in terms of improved general well-being, reduced motor tension and enhanced activity levels. … [BOP] is now recommended [by NICE], amongst other*

*non-verbal/arts therapies, as the treatment
of choice for chronic schizophrenia patients
with predominant negative symptoms.*
(Rohricht, 2012, pp. 274–275)

There is good reason to expect that body psychotherapy will in time be demonstrated to have wide-ranging value as a therapy modality. As already noted, it can lean on a great deal of research support from contemporary neuroscience. While neuroscience undoubtedly validates body psychotherapy, there is less reason to think that it will improve the work itself, which rests firmly on clinical experience.

SUGGESTED READING

Conger, J. P. (1994). *The Body in Recovery: Somatic Psychotherapy and the Self*. Berkeley, CA: Frog.
Corrigall, J., Payne, H., & Wilkinson, H. (Eds.) (2006). *About A Body: Working with the Embodied Mind in Psychotherapy*. London: Routledge.

Heckler, R. S. (1985). *The Anatomy of Change: East/West Approaches to Bodymind Therapy.* Boston, MA: Shambhala.

Johnson, D. H. (Ed.) (1997). *Groundworks: Narratives of Embodiment.* Berkeley, CA: North Atlantic.

Totton, N. (2003). *Body Psychotherapy: An Introduction.* Maidenhead, UK: Open University Press.

Totton, N. (2015). *Embodied Relating: The Ground of Psychotherapy.* London: Karnac/Routledge.

Young, C. (Ed.) (2012). *About the Science of Body Psychotherapy.* Stow, Galashiels, UK: Body Psychotherapy Publications.

Young, C. (Ed.) (2018). *About Touch in Body Psychotherapy: Vol. 1.* Stow, Galashiels, UK: Body Psychotherapy Publications.

4

PROBLEMS, DEBATES, CONTROVERSIES, FUTURES

So far, I have tried as much as possible to clarify the history, present status, theories, and techniques of body psychotherapy. In this final chapter I will address what is unclear, uncertain, undecided, and open to interpretation; and sketch some alternative visions as to the future of body psychotherapy.

Chapter 4

MINIMUM DEFINITION

As the previous chapter showed, body psychotherapists have a wide range of techniques and
approaches available to them, many of which are
very unusual in a psychotherapeutic context – for
example, breathwork, massage, and other physical
interventions, lying down, standing up, and moving
around. So far I have described BP in terms of its
range of options; but could one also offer a minimal
definition – the necessary and sufficient conditions
for someone to call themself a body psychotherapy
practitioner rather than a psychotherapist with an
interest in embodiment?

There are very different views on this within
the field, boiling down to two main positions both
of which I feel have some merit. One of these argues that anyone is a body psychotherapist who
consistently tracks their own embodied process
as they sit with a client, and looks for connections
with what is happening in the therapeutic interaction (Totton, 2015, Ch. 11). The other accepts

that this is a *necessary* condition, but argues that it is only *sufficient* when supported by specialist training, and that suggesting otherwise risks undermining our modality completely.

Which of these is right probably depends at least in part on the individual practitioner. Certainly it is hard, in a largely body-denying culture, to achieve and maintain a sufficient focus on the embodied relationship; and a BP training is dedicated to achieving this – and also to addressing the important question, what next? Having linked my embodied process to what the client is discussing, what do I do about it? Trained body psychotherapists generally have more and different answers to this question.

DIFFERENCE AND NORMALITY

Writing this little book has been very useful for me because it has encouraged me to revisit and reconsider the field afresh, and to ask myself whether everything I see is fit for purpose in 2020. In at least one area, my answer has to be "no". BP has not yet shaken off its historic tendency towards normativity: the assumption of – or worse, the aspiration towards – the "normal" body. In this we are challenged, as in so many other aspects of our current culture, to look deeply at our attitudes towards difference, and at the ways in which we exclude and ignore those whom we experience as different.

Body psychotherapy is unavoidably right at the heart of this matter, simply because it is concerned with bodies. Many dimensions of bodily difference are coded for difference in power and status, including gender, skin colour, able-bodiedness, age, size, and conventional attractiveness. In its attitudes to this, BP has the power, and the responsibility, to influence society. So far it has shown little interest in acting positively in this arena – which means that by default its influence is negative, reinforcing traditional discriminations by not challenging them.

I will take disability as an example here,

because it is still perhaps the area of bodily discrimination where both BP and society are least conscious and most habitual. Here are extracts from a fairly typical, everyday exercise that most BP practitioners might use with individuals or groups to ground bodily awareness:

> *Bring your awareness to your feet, and feel their contact with the ground … Let your attention go into the sounds you can hear in the room … Lift your arms as high as you can … Look around and notice the colours … Follow your breath as it moves in and out of your body ….*

What I have been saying should have cued you into noticing the assumptions of able-bodiedness built into these very "ordinary" instructions. But would you have noticed otherwise?

Of course any therapist would realise, if there was a disabled person in a group, that they must tell the person they could drop out of the exercise (itself discriminatory and humiliating), or rethink what they were doing. But *only* if a disabled person was present – suggesting a clear double standard. I frequently experience the same lazy assumptions and "just-in-time sensitivity" around ethnicity, queerness, transgender, and other issues. Something far more radical is called for, in line with the changes that society as a whole is being challenged to make: a recasting of the work we do, and the way we think, which is orders of magnitude more inclusive than is currently the case. How do we find a way of starting out from what we really do all have in common – and addressing our differences without ranking them for value?

JOINING THE RESISTANCE: HOW POLITICAL IS BODY PSYCHOTHERAPY?

As Don Hanlon Johnson writes:

> *Underlying the various techniques and schools [of BP], one finds a desire to regain*

> *an intimate connect with bodily processes:*
> *breath, movement impulses, balance and*
> *sensibility. In that shared impulse, this*
> *community is best understood within a*
> *much broader movement of resistance to*
> *the West's long history of denigrating the*
> *value of the human body and the natural*
> *environment.*
> (1995, p. xvi)

This alignment with countercultural values was very much part and parcel of my own and many other people's initial engagement with body psychotherapy. I first encountered Reich in political contexts in the 1960s and 1970s, and this formed part of the attraction. But how far, if at all, is the alignment intrinsic to body psychotherapy, rather than a short-term historical phenomenon?

Reich himself is actually an interesting test case: during the period when he was developing his orientation to the body, he was deeply committed to revolutionary left politics, and saw several direct and crucial links between the two. Body psychotherapy, he felt, liberated the energy that was repressed under capitalism; this made people much harder to control, and frequently led them to leave jobs they hated or relationships that were unsatisfying. He wrote a brilliant book (1970) applying body psychotherapy ideas to an analysis of the rise of fascism in Germany.

Reich saw the projects of social and personal liberation as essentially united – and in this he directly influenced the 1960s view that "the personal is political". Later in his life, however, and in some of his posthumous influence, Reich seemed to move a lot closer to American libertarian right-wing views, including a paranoia about "Red Fascists". We can justifiably ascribe some of this shift to Reich's increasing instability under the stress of very real persecution; but it still challenges any easy assumption about the politics of BP.

Although many of the older generation of BP practitioners have similar attitudes to mine, I see the potential for different threads to emerge in the younger generation: body psychotherapy could become more associated with Foucault's "care of the self" (see Chapter 2), taking on a narcissistic and apolitical tone and blending with "gym culture". But really there is no such thing as the "apolitical": it is always a cloak for conservative or reactionary attitudes, generally linked to the sort of normativity I discussed above – "This is just the way things are, always have been, always will be". And care of the self can easily blend into *discipline* of the self. As I have written elsewhere:

> *From one point of view, body psychotherapy is a project of self-care, where the therapist facilitates the client in achieving greater ease, relaxation, self-esteem, happiness, and so on. At the same time, though, body psychotherapy can easily operate as the transmission belt for a whole array of social demands on the individual, some of which we perhaps first encounter at primary school: Stand up straight! Breathe!*

Speak up! Work hard! Relate well to others! Feel good about yourself!
(Totton, 2015, p. 68)

A TOUCHY ISSUE

Every time I speak publicly as a body psychotherapist, every time I edit a book or symposium on the subject, I will probably be asked about touch. Like many other BP practitioners, I get tired of justifying the use of touch in psychotherapy! This can drain energy so that my arguments become superficial; which is a shame, because outside our small BP circle the doubts are very real.

The main, though not the only, reason for this is clearly that in our society touch tends to be sexualised (and hence, like sex, commodified). On the whole, we don't touch each other very much; and when we do, it is generally in one of three contexts – parenting and other family relationships, physical or medical care, or sexual love. The more sophisticated critiques of therapeutic touching rightly point out that none of these contexts can be evoked in psychotherapy without consequences of one kind or another. But it is clear that much of the charge around the issue derives from the perceived sexual overtones that associate touch in body psychotherapy with "inappropriateness".

There is much to question in this. The analytic community, who (unlike the young Freud) abstain most rigorously from touch, are the first to say that the most apparently "innocent" acts can be sexualised in a therapeutic context; yet the only ones actually forbidden are those most transparent for discussion. On the other hand, I have heard an analyst seriously propose that if one was ushering a patient upstairs to the therapy room and they slipped on the stairs, it would be better to let them fall than to steady them with a hand on the elbow. I don't think this is agreed policy, but it shows the scale of the taboo, which has influenced the whole of psychotherapy. Yet the most extreme feelings of love and attraction are welcomed into the therapy relationship – so long as they are expressed only verbally. Perhaps it is useful to recast the debate as being centrally about power rather than about sexuality (Lidy Evertson, personal communication). We can assert power over another person as strongly by *withholding* touch as by giving it, and each can be equally unwelcome.

Certainly, practitioners need to be trained in the use of touch and its implications – just as they need to be trained in all therapeutic techniques. One needs to know when *not* to touch. And certainly, no therapists should use touch unless they feel comfortable with it; and many of those drawn to train as therapists, it seems, are the sort of people who don't feel comfortable with touch. However, the majority of body psychotherapists are in no doubt of its value for many clients, whether as comfort and reassurance, as a way of exploring contact issues, as a way of provoking repressed feelings and impulses, or as a skilled and subtle conversation with the body. As I have written elsewhere, I have always had clients I don't touch often or at all; but "I cannot imagine working without the possibility of touch as an active, continuous and creative element in my practice" (Totton, 2006, p. 161).

BODY PSYCHOTHERAPY AND DANCE MOVEMENT PSYCHOTHERAPY

The relationship between BP and Dance Movement Psychotherapy (DMP) has long been problematic. The two can be seen as versions of the same thing: both work psychotherapeutically with the body and its impulses. It is true that BP specialises in what one might call "the body at rest", and DMP in "the body in motion"; but neither is exclusive of the other, and there are few BP practitioners who never work with movement or DMP practitioners who never work with stillness. Each has its own body of theoretical understandings, but surely both would gain from pooling their knowledge.

It is interesting and perhaps significant that most of the central figures in the development of DMP are women, while in BP most are men. This parallels the historical pairing between several prominent male BP practitioners and their DMP wives or partners. It is only one of several ways in which the two modalities seem to exist complementarily. DMP has evolved as primarily group work, BP as primarily one-to-one; DMP sees itself as a creative arts therapy while BP does not; DMP commonly works in the UK within the NHS, with the elderly, children, people defined as mentally ill, and those with learning difficulties, and is regulated by the Health and Care Professions Council; BP has barely the slightest foothold in the NHS, and very little presence in agencies of any kind, operating mostly in private practice and hence with relatively high-functioning clients from the general population.

I want to thank Roz Carroll (personal communication) for helping me clarify my perception of the relationship between the two approaches, and for supporting my belief that both would gain from a closer relationship. There has since 2006 been a peer-reviewed international *Journal of Body, Movement and Dance in Psychotherapy*, which is perhaps an encouraging sign of an eventual rapprochement. The USABP accepts DMP as a body psychotherapy modality – which is of course not quite the same as accepting it as equal but different.

SUSTAINABILITY

On top of all the other factors limiting the prevalence of body psychotherapy, it is quite hard for its practitioners to sustain. To do it properly demands very intense contact with the client, and therefore also with oneself. In all therapy, of course, one needs to be highly aware of the other's, and one's own, thoughts and feelings; but BP adds to this an awareness of both parties' embodiment as it waxes and wanes, twists and turns through different states – an awareness that finds parallels perhaps only in that between lovers, or between a baby and its carer. Yet we cannot *sink into* this embodied field in the way a lover or a mother might do: our awareness needs at the same time to be constantly alert, critical, thoughtful.

So it is no surprise that many trained body psychotherapists find themselves over time less and less working directly with embodiment. There is a particular point of balance that one needs to find and maintain in order to do this work. Something similar is true for all psychotherapy, I think – it is after all a very peculiar occupation, whose practitioners need to be able to manage, and even to enjoy, intense regular contact with someone who after an hour *goes away*. But BP seems to be even more demanding; and whether we can find the balance required is probably a matter of constitution and development, on which training can have only a limited effect.

WILL BODY PSYCHOTHERAPY SURVIVE AS A DISTINCT MODALITY?

Even after leaving its bunker in the 1990s, BP has continued to be something of an oddity and an exception in the general field of psychotherapy. Things that most modalities regard as unusual or even unacceptable – touching clients, moving around in the room, bringing in the client's or one's own physical sensations – are for body psychotherapy everyday matters. There are real questions, especially given the constant pressure towards regulation and monitoring, as to how long this state of exception can be maintained.

There are several possible ways in which things could change. BP could be forced back into the bunker, excluded from recognition by the psychotherapy establishment. Or it could be pressured into giving up its unruly habits and restricting itself to what I have heard called "passive embodiment" – that is, working quietly with the practitioner's own embodied response but not directly engaging with that of the client. Since there is wide interest in this sort of approach among verbally oriented practitioners, we might end up with everybody being a *bit* of a body psychotherapist – but not enough to frighten the horses.

Such an outcome would mean losing the biggest gift that body psychotherapy has to offer: a different basic assumption about human beings and about psychotherapy, which grounds our experience and our problems in our embodiment. As Don Hanlon Johnson says in the passage quoted above, this understanding puts body psychotherapy firmly on the side of the new culture that is struggling for hegemony. Through the body, we can come back home; and as a result gain access to an ecosystemic perspective that respects life in all its forms, including our own.

I therefore maintain, as Gramsci says, an optimism of the will, however pessimistic my intellect may be about the future of body psychotherapy. Psychotherapy as a whole is faced with enormous challenges as to whether it can maintain the wild, unruly, and provocative sides of its nature in the face of a social trend towards normality, surveillance, and control. It is possible that body psychotherapy, the wildest of the bunch, may have an important role in this project of resistance.

SUGGESTED READING

Caldwell, C., & Leighton, L. B. (Eds.) (2018). *Oppression and the Body: Roots, Resistance, and Resolutions*. Berkeley, CA: North Atlantic.

Galton, G. (2006). *Touch Papers: Dialogues on Touch in the Psychoanalytic Space*. London: Karnac/Routledge.

Johnson, R. (2018). *Embodied Social Justice.* London: Routledge.

Reich, W. (1970). *The Mass Psychology of Fascism*. London: Penguin, 1975.

Totton, N. (2011). *Wild Therapy: Undomesticating Inner and Outer Worlds.* Ross-on-Wye, UK: PCCS Books.

REFERENCES

Note: Works referred to only in the Suggested Reading are not listed below.

Aron, L. (1998). Introduction: The body in drive and relational models. In: L. Aron & F. S. Anderson (Eds.), *Relational Perspectives on the Body* (pp. xix–xxviii). New York: Routledge.

Asheri, S. (2009). To touch or not to touch: A relational body psychotherapy perspective. In: L. Hartley (Ed.), *Contemporary Body Psychotherapy: The Chiron Approach* (pp. 106–120). London: Routledge.

Asheri, S. (2018). Stepping into the void. In: J. Yellin & O. B. Epstein (Eds.), *Terror Within and Without: Attachment and Disintegration: Clinical Work on the Edge* (pp. 73–81). Abingdon, UK: Routledge,.

Baker, E. F. (1967). *Man in the Trap: The Causes of Blocked Sexual Energy.* New York: Avon Books. [Reprinted New York: Collier, 1980.]

Balint, M. (1950). Changing therapeutical aims and techniques in psycho-analysis. *International Journal of Psychoanalysis,* 31: 117–124 .

Barratt, B. B. (2010). *The Emergence of Somatic Psychology and Bodymind Therapy.* London: Palgrave Macmillan.

Boadella, D. (1987). *Lifestreams: An Introduction to Biosynthesis.* London: Routledge & Kegan Paul.

Boston Change Process Study Group (2010). *Change in Psychotherapy: A Unifying Paradigm.* New York: W. W. Norton.

Boyesen, E. (1980). The essence of energy distribution. In: *The Collected Papers of Biodynamic Psychology, Volumes 1 and 2* (pp. 102–104). London: Biodynamic Psychology Publications.

Budgeon, S. (2003). Identity as embodied event. *Body and Society,* 9: 35–55.

Carroll, R. (2005). Neuroscience and "the law of the self": the autonomic nervous system updated, re-mapped and in relationship.

In: N. Totton (Ed.), *New Dimensions in Body Psychotherapy* (pp. 13–29). Maidenhead, UK: Open University Press.

Carroll, R. (2009). Self-regulation: an evolving concept at the heart of body psychotherapy. In: L. Hartley (Ed.), *Contemporary Body Psychotherapy: The Chiron Approach* (pp. 89–105). London: Routledge.

Carroll, R. (2012). "At the border between chaos and order": What psychotherapy and neuroscience have in common. In: C. Young (Ed.), *About the Science of Body Psychotherapy* (pp. 3–26). Stow, Galashiels, UK: Body Psychotherapy Publications.

Carroll, R. (2014). Four relational modes of attending to the body in psychotherapy. In: K. White (Ed.), *Talking Bodies: How Do We Integrate Working with the Body in Psychotherapy from an Attachment and Relational Perspective?* (pp. 11–40). London: Karnac.

Chiel, H. J., & Beer, R. D. (1997). The brain has a body: Adaptive behavior emerges from interactions of nervous system, body and environment. *Trends in Neuroscience*, 20: 553–557.

Cohen, D. (1995). *An Introduction to Craniosacral Therapy: Anatomy, Function, and Treatment*. Berkeley, CA: North Atlantic.

Conger, J. P. (1994). *The Body in Recovery: Somatic Psychotherapy and the Self.* Berkeley, CA: Frog.

Cornell. W. F. (2009a). Stranger to desire: Entering the erotic field. *Studies in Gender and Sexuality*, 10: 75–92.

Cornell, W. F. (2009b). Response to Shapiro's discussion. *Studies in Gender and Sexuality*, 10: 104–111.

Cornell, W. F. (2015). *Somatic Experience in Psychoanalysis and Psychotherapy*. London: Routledge.

Damasio, A. (1994). *Descartes' Error: Emotion, Reason and the Human Brain*. London: PaperMac.

Damasio, A. (2000). *The Feeling of What Happens: Body, Emotion and the Making of Consciousness*. London: Heinemann.

Eigen, M. (1993). *The Electrified Tightrope*. Northvale, NJ: Jason Aronson.

Ferenczi, S. (1933). Confusion of tongues between adults and the child (the language of tenderness and of passion). In: J. Borossa (Ed.),

Ferenczi: Selected Writings (pp. 293 –303). London: Penguin.

Ferenczi, S. (1988). *The Clinical Diary.* J. Dupont (Ed.) London: Harvard University Press.

Finlay, L. (2011). *Phenomenology for Therapists: Researching the Lived World.* Oxford: Wiley-Blackwell.

Fischer, C., & Dolezal L. (Eds.) (2018). *New Feminist Perspectives on Embodiment: Breaking Feminist Waves.* London: Palgrave Macmillan.

Fogel, A. (2013). *Body Sense: The Science and Practice of Embodied Self-Awareness.* New York: W. W. Norton.

Fournier, V. (2002). Fleshing out gender: Crafting gender identity on women's bodies. *Body and Society*, 8: 55–77.

Freud, S. (1923b). *The Ego and the Id. S. E., 19*: pp. 3–68. London: Hogarth.

Freud, S. (1926d). *Inhibitions, Symptoms and Anxiety. S. E., 20*: pp. 77–178. London: Hogarth.

Freud, S., & Breuer, J. (1895d). *Studies on Hysteria. S. E., 2*. London: Hogarth.

Gendlin, E. T. (1998). *Focusing-Oriented Psychotherapy: A Manual of the Experiential Method.* New York: Guilford Press.

Geuter, U., Heller, M. C., & Weaver, J. O. (2010). Elsa Gindler and her influence on Wilhelm Reich and body psychotherapy. *Body, Movement and Dance in Psychotherapy*, 5(1): 59–73.

Greenberg, J. R., & Mitchell, S. A. (1983). *Object Relations in Psychoanalytic Theory.* London: Harvard University Press.

Groddeck, G. (1931). Massage and psychotherapy. In: L. Schacht (Ed.), *The Meaning of Illness: Selected Psychoanalytic Writings by Georg Groddeck* (pp. 235–240). London: Maresfield Library, 1977.

Grof, S. (1975). *Realms of the Human Unconscious.* London: Souvenir Press.

Grossinger, R. (1995). *Planet Medicine.* 6th edition. 2 vols. Berkeley, CA: North Atlantic.

Hartley, L. (Ed.) (2009). *Contemporary Body Psychotherapy: The Chiron Approach.* London: Routledge.

Heckler, R. S. (1984). *The Anatomy of Change: East/West Ap-*

proaches to Bodymind Therapy. Boston, MA: Shambhala.

Heller, M. (2012). *Body Psychotherapy: History, Concepts, and Methods*. New York: W. W. Norton.

Huffer, L. (2010). *Mad for Foucault: Rethinking the Foundations of Queer Theory*. New York: Columbia University Press.

Johnson, D. H. (1995). *Bone, Breath and Gesture: Practices of Embodiment*. Berkeley, CA: North Atlantic.

Johnson, D. H. (2000). "Intricate tactile sensitivity." *Progress in Brain Research*, 122: 479–490.

Jones, E. E. (1993). Introduction to special section: Single-case research in psychotherapy. *Journal of Consulting and Clinical Psychology*, 61(3): 371–372.

Kauffman, S. (1995). *At Home in the Universe: The Search for Laws of Self-Organization and Complexity*. Oxford: Oxford University Press.

Keleman, S (1975). *Your Body Speaks Its Mind*. Berkeley, CA: Center Press.

Kelley, C. R. (1974). *Education in Feeling and Purpose*, 2nd Edition. Santa Monica, CA: Radix Institute.

Kurtz, R. (1985). *Hakomi Therapy*. 2nd edition. Boulder, CO: Hakomi Institute.

Labworth, Y., & Wilson, W. (2000). Biosynthesis. *The Fulcrum*, 19: 16–19.

Levine, P. A. (1997). *Waking the Tiger: Healing Trauma*. Berkeley, CA: North Atlantic.

Lowen, A. (1976a). *Bioenergetics*. London: Penguin.

Lowen, A. (1976b). Bio-energetic analysis. In: D. Boadella (Ed.), *In the Wake of Reich* (pp. 181–191). London: Coventure.

Lowen, A. (1977). *The Way to Vibrant Health: A Manual of Bioenergetic Exercises*. New York: Harper Colophon.

Marcher, L., & Fich, S. (2010). *Body Encyclopedia: A Guide to the Psychological Functions of the Muscular System*. Berkeley, CA: North Atlantic.

Masson, J. (Ed.) (1985). *The Complete Letters of Sigmund Freud to Wilhelm Fliess*. London: Belknap Press.

May, J. M. (2005). The outcome of body psychotherapy. *USA Body Psychotherapy Journal*, 4: 98–120.

Mindell, A. (1985). *River's Way: The Process Science of Dreambody.* London: Penguin Arkana.

Mitchell, S. A. (2000). *Relationality: From Attachment to Intersubjectivity.* London: Analytic Press.

Nissen, T., & Wynn, R. (2014). The clinical case report: a review of its merits and limitations. *BMC Research Notes*, 7: 264.

Ogden, P., Minton, K., & Paine, C. (2006). *Trauma and the Body: A Sensorimotor Approach to Psychotherapy.* New York: W. W. Norton.

Painter, J. W. (1984). *Deep Bodywork and Personal Development: Harmonizing Our Bodies, Emotions and Thoughts.* Mill Valley, CA: Center for Release and Integration.

Perls, F., Hefferline, R. F., & Goodman, P. (1951). *Gestalt Therapy: Excitement and Growth in the Human Personality.* New York: Julian Press. [Reprinted London: Penguin, 1973.]

Piers, C. (2000). Character as self-organizing complexity. *Psychoanalysis and Contemporary Thought*, 23(1): 3–34.

Porges, S. W. (2005). The role of social engagement in attachment and bonding: a phylogenetic perspective. In: C. S. Carter, L. Ahnert, K. E. Grossman, S. B. Hrdy, M. E. Lamb, S. W. Porges, & N. Sachser (Eds.), *Attachment and Bonding: A New Synthesis* (pp. 33 –54). Cambridge, MA: MIT Press.

Porges, S. W. (2011). *The Polyvagal Theory: Neurophysiological Foundations of Emotions, Attachment, Communication, and Self-Regulation.* New York: W. W. Norton.

Porges, S. W., & Dana, D. A. (2018). *Clinical Applications of the Polyvagal Theory: The Emergence of Polyvagal-Informed Therapies.* New York: W. W. Norton.

Raknes, O. (1971). *Wilhelm Reich and Orgonomy: The Controversial Theory of Life Energy.* Baltimore, MD: Penguin.

Reich, W. (1970). *The Mass Psychology of Fascism.* New York: Farrar, Straus and Giroux. [Original German publication 1945; this translation reprinted London: Penguin, 1975.]

Reich, W. (1972). *Character Analysis.* 3rd enlarged edition. New York: Farrar, Straus and Giroux. [Original German publication of Parts I and II, 1933.]

References

Reich, W. (1973). *The Function of the Orgasm*. New York: Farrar, Straus & Giroux. First published in English in 1942. Tr. Vincent R Carfagno.

Rohricht, F. (2009). Body-oriented psychotherapy – the state of the art in empirical research and evidence based practice: A clinical perspective. *Journal of Body, Movement and Dance in Psychotherapy*, 4(2): 135–156.

Rohricht, F. (2012). Body-oriented psychotherapy – the state of the art in empirical research and evidence based practice: A clinical perspective [revised and expanded version]. In: C. Young (Ed.), *About the Science of Body Psychotherapy* (pp. 251–289). Stow, Galashiels, UK: Body Psychotherapy Publications.

Rosenberg, J. L., & Rand, M. L. (1985). *Body, Self, and Soul: Sustaining Integration*. Atlanta, GA: Humanics,

Rothschild, B. (2000). *The Body Remembers: The Psychophysiology of Trauma and Trauma Treatment*. New York: W. W. Norton.

Schore, A. N. (1994). *Regulation and the Origin of the Self: The Neurobiology of Emotional Development*. Mahwah, NJ: Lawrence Erlbaum.

Shapiro, S. A. (2009). A rush to action: Embodiment, the analyst's subjectivity, and the interpersonal experience. *Studies in Gender and Sexuality*, 10: 93–103.

Soth, M. (2005). Embodied countertransference. In: N. Totton (Ed.), *New Dimensions in Body Psychotherapy* (pp. 40–55). Maidenhead, UK: Open University Press.

Soth, M. (2006). What therapeutic hope for a subjective mind in an objectified body? In: J. Corrigall, H. Payne, & H. Wilkinson (Eds.), *About a Body: Working with the Embodied Mind in Psychotherapy* (pp. 111–131). London: Routledge.

Soth, M. (2009). From humanistic holism via the "integrative project" towards integral-relational body psychotherapy. In: L. Hartley (Ed.), *Contemporary Body Psychotherapy: The Chiron Approach* (pp. 64–88). London: Routledge.

Southgate, J. (1980). *Basic dimensions of character analysis. Energy and Character*, 11(1): 48–65.

References

Stern, D. N. (1985). *The Interpersonal World of the Infant.* New York: Basic Books.

Totton, N. (1998). *The Water in the Glass: Body and Mind in Psychoanalysis.* London: Rebus Press/Karnac.

Totton, N. (2002). Foreign bodies: Recovering the history of body psychotherapy. In: T. Staunton (Ed.), *Body Psychotherapy* (pp. 7–26). London: Brunner-Routledge.

Totton, N. (2003). *Body Psychotherapy: An Introduction.* Maidenhead, UK: Open University Press.

Totton, N. (2006). A body psychotherapist's approach to touch. In: G. Galton (Ed.), *Touch Papers: Dialogues on Touch in the Psychoanalytic Space* (pp. 145–161). London: Karnac/Routledge.

Totton, N. (2007). *Embodied relating. In: Not A Tame Lion: Writings on Therapy in its Social and Political Context* (pp. 141–149). Ross-on-Wye, UK: PCCS Books, 2012.

Totton, N. (2011). *Wild Therapy: Undomesticating Our Inner and Outer Worlds.* Ross-on-Wye, UK: PCCS Books.

Totton, N. (2015). *Embodied Relating: The Ground of Psychotherapy.* London: Karnac/Routledge.

Totton, N., & Edmondson, E. (2009). *Reichian Growth Work: Melting the Blocks to Life and Love.* 2nd edition. Ross-on-Wye, UK: PCCS Books.

Totton, N., & Jacobs, M. (2001). *Character and Personality Types.* Maidenhead, UK: Open University Press.

Trevarthen, C., & Aitken, K. J. (2001). Infant intersubjectivity: Research, theory and clinical applications. *Journal of Child Psychology and Psychiatry,* 42(1): 3–48.

Van der Kolk, B. (2014). *The Body Keeps the Score: Mind, Brain and Body in the Transformation of Trauma.* New York: Viking.

Winnicott, D. W. (1949). Mind and its relation to the psyche-soma. In: *Through Paediatrics to Psychoanalysis: Collected Papers* (pp. 243–254). London: Karnac, 1987.

Young, C. (Ed.) (2012). *About the Science of Body Psychotherapy.* Stow, Galashiels, UK: Body Psychotherapy Publications.

INDEX

abledness, disability, 7, 65, 83, 136-7
abreaction, 10
abuse, sexual, 13
Adjustment model of body
    psychotherapy, 4, 5-9, 10, 20
aggression, 9, 99
armour, armouring 35, 37, 40, 52,
    54-5, 100-2, 106, 118
    see character armour, muscular
      armour
Asheri, Shoshi, 22, 69
attachment, 77, 92
attractors, 78, 105
Autonomic Nervous System (ANS),
    43, 73, 109-12, 124

biodynamic therapy, 54, 122
Bioenergetics, 40, 55, 122
Biosynthesis, 56, 109
birth, 38, 58f, 115
blocks, energetic, 5f, 42, 103, 116,
    121-3, 125
Boadella, David, 40, 56, 109, 115
bodymind, 9, 14, 40, 59, 66
    unity, 2, 61, 94-5, 100
    split, 1, 16, 43-4
bodynamics, 54, 101
body psychotherapy
    models, 4-20
    organisations, 62-3, 65, 85
    professional aspects,62, 72, 87-
      92, 127
    see also European Association
      for Body Psychotherapy
'Body Psychotherapy 1.0', 22, 72, 83
'Body Psychotherapy 2.0', 22, 65
bonding, social, 76-7
Boston Change Process Study
    Group (BCPSG), 67-8

Boyesen, Gerda, 54, 122
brain, 74, 84, 110
breath, 8, 13, 31, 32-3, 35-6, 42, 57,
    59, 74, 100, 110, 122-6, 133,
    136, 138, 140

capitalism, 37, 139
Carroll, Roz, 22, 69, 72, 80, 84,
    112, 145
Carter, Sue, 76
Central Nervous System (CNS),
    110-11, 124
centring, 106-7, 109
    see also facing, grounding,
      skying
channels of experience, 37, 47, 60,
    80, 109, 120
character, 9, 15, 35-7, 40, 47-9, 53,
    76, 100, 101-5, 106, 115
    armour, 35, 100, 101
charge, 47, 59, 70, 96, 142
    see also discharge, energy
chi, 98
Chiron Centre, 63
cognition, cognitive science
    66, 82, 88, 92, 102, 148
communism, 38
complexity, 21, 66, 77, 105
Conger, John P, 94, 106, 130
contact, 51, 69, 75, 77, 106, 108f,
    114, 117-22, 136, 143, 146-7
    eye, 75, 109
    ground, 108, 136
    gut, 106
    heart, 75
    in therapy, 117-22
    sky/cosmos, 108
    voice, 109
    see also presence, touch

Index

contactlessness, 118
core, 41, 106-7
core beliefs, 104
Cornell, William, 69
cosmos, 39, 53-4, 108

Damasio, Anthony, 61
Dance Movement Psychotherapy
    (DMP), 23, 30, 57, 61, 144-5
desire, 5, 29, 34, 36-7, 43, 69, 89,
    101, 137
disability, see abledness
discharge, 4, 9-13, 11, 20, 29, 43,
    58, 113
    see also charge
dissociation, 10, 37, 76
    see also fight-flight-freeze,
        trauma
drives, 28, 38, 68, 96

ecology, 40
    see also environment, other-
        than-human
edges 15, 23p., 57, 60, 67-8, 74, 78,
    81, 91-2, 96, 116, 130-1, 144,
    150
Edmondson, Em, 108
Emotional Freedom Technique
    (EFT), 11
ego, 1, 7, 28f, 35, 43-4, 100, 124
    'spastic ego', 44
embodied relational paradigm,
    69-71
embodiment, 2-4, 7, 15, 17, 23f, 28,
    36, 51, 60, 62, 65-6, 67-9,
    70, 81-2, 84-5, 91-2, 94, 100,
    107, 111, 118-19, 121, 130-
    1, 133-4, 146-7, 150
    and character, 102-4
    'passive embodiment', 148
    the therapist's, 17-18, 70-1, 146,
    148
energy, 5, 8, 37, 40, 42-3, 54-5,
    74, 76, 78, 96-8, 103, 105,
        106-7, 108, 119, 122-3, 125,
        139, 141
    bound, 29, 43
environment, 81, 84, 138
    see also ecology, other-than-
        human
ethnicity, 26, 83, 135
European Association for Body
    Psychotherapy (EABP), 86-8
Evertson, Lidy, 22, 143
exaptation, 77
expression, expressiveness
    emotional, 9f, 35, 100, 110-11,
        125
    facial, 30, 36, 44-7, 49, 75, 111
    of core beliefs, 104
    vocal, 99, 111
    bodily, 6, 17, 31, 34-5, 36-7, 80,
        97, 99-100, 104, 125
Eye Movement Desensitization and
    Reprocessing (EMDR), 11

facing, 75, 106, 109
    see also grounding, centring,
        skying
fascism, 139, 150
feminism, 83
Ferenczi, Sandor, 11, 27, 29f, 32,
    36-7
fight-flight-freeze, 74, 76-7
    see also dissociation, trauma
Focusing, 57-8
    see also Gendlin, Eugene
Foucault, Michel, 82-3, 140
    see also technologies of the self
Freud, Sigmund, 9, 21, 26-30, 32-3,
    35, 39, 41-3, 56, 58, 68, 96,
    142
    see also psychoanalysis
functional identity of soma and
    psyche, 95, 106-7

gender, 7, 32, 83, 135, 137, 144
Gendlin, Eugene, 57-8

Index

see also focusing
Gestalt psychotherapy, 31, 56, 118
    see also Perls, Fritz
Gibson, James and Eleanor, 81
Gindler, Elsa, 31-3
Groddeck, Georg, 30, 32
Grof, Stanislav, 59
    see also Holotropic Breathwork
Grossinger, Richard, 25, 63
grounding, 8, 106-9, 136
    vertical and horizontal, 107-8
    see also ungroundedness,
      centring, facing, skying
Gymnastik, 31

Hakomi Method, 56
    see also Kurtz, Ron
Heckler,Richard Strozzi, 98, 106-7,
    118-19, 131
Heller, Michel, 25, 32-3
heterosexuality 41, 56
    see also queer
Holotropic Breathwork, 57, 59
    see also Grof, Stanislav
human potential movement, 61
humanistic psychotherapy, 40-2,
    105
hyperventilation, 125-6
hysteria, 27

id, 43
implicit relational knowing, 68
infant development, 66, 79
intricate tactile sensitivity (ITS),
    120-2
involuntary expression, 30, 45, 108,
    123-4

Janov, Arthur, 58
    see also primal therapy
Johnson, Don Hanlon, 120f, 131,
    137, 149-50
Jung, Carl, 26, 60

Keleman, Stanley, 14
Kelley, Charles, 40, 56, 97
    see also Radix
Kurtz, Ron, 14
    see also Hakomi Method

Levine, Peter, 11, 24
libido, 34, 39, 42, 96
Lindenberg, Elsa, 31-2
Lowen, Alexander, 5f, 40, 55, 97,
    107-8, 111, 122
    see also bioenergetics

Merleau-Ponty, Maurice, 81
    see also phenomenology
Mindell, Arnold, 15, 24, 59-60
minimum definition of body
    psychotherapy,   133
Mitchell, Stephen, 67
motor functions, 37, 71, 110, 129
musculature, 10, 13, 34p-6, 42-4,
    46, 48, 51, 74-5, 100-1, 107,
    116, 122-3, 125-6
muscular armour, armouring, 35,
    100
    see also character armour

nonlinear dynamic systems (NDS),
    77-8
neuroscience, 61, 66, 71-5, 80-1, 84,
    112, 130
neurosis, 6, 15, 42-3, 56
'normality', 6, 14, 56, 74, 109,
    134-5, 149

'one-person psychotherapy', 67-8
    see also 'two-person
      psychotherapy'
orgone, 54, 96-8
orgonomy, 39, 54-6, 95
orgonomic funtionalism, 95
other-than-human, the, 53, 85
    see also ecology, environment

Index

parasympathetic nervous
    system, 73-4, 76-7, 106, 111
    see also sympathetic nervous
    system, autonomic nervous
    system
perinatal experience, 58-9
    see also birth
Perls, Fritz, 15, 26, 31, 56, 118
    see also Gestalt therapy
phenomenology, 66, 81, 128
    see also Merleau-Ponty, Maurice
pleasure, 3, 10, 29, 41, 51, 113
politics, 37f, 62, 82-3, 104, 127,
    137-8
polyvagal theory, 73, 77, 91, 111
    see also Porges, Stephen, social
    engagement system
Porges, Stephen, 73-4, 109-11
prana, 98
presence, 119-20
primal therapy, 58-9
    see also Janov, Arthur
Process model of body
    psychotherapy, 4, 13-17,
    37, 133
Process Oriented Psychology (POP,
    processwork), 57, 59-60
psychoanalysis, 26, 28, 30, 33f, 37-
    40, 45, 63, 66-7, 69, 72, 81,
    111, 124, 150
    see also Freud
Post Traumatic Stress Disorder
    (PTSD), 11, 113

queer, 83, 137

Radix 56, 96
    see also Kelley, Charles
Raknes, Ola, 54, 114
Rand, Marjorie, 116-17
Rank, Otto, 58
Randomised Control Trials (RCTs),
    127-8
regression, 58

Reich, Wilhelm, 9f, 17, 26, 30-2,
    33-55, 57, 63, 69, 80, 95-6,
    98-104, 108-9, 111-14, 116,
    118, 122-3, 138-9, 150
relationality, 58, 72, 75-7, 79-80, 84,
    86, 91, 105, 108, 112, 118
Relational model of body
    psychotherapy, 4, 17-20
    see also embodied-relational
    paradigm
relational psychoanalysis, 67-9, 91-2
relationship, therapeutic, 20, 37, 58,
    67, 70, 124, 134, 142
    see also structural coupling
repression, 9, 29, 34, 37-8, 100-1
research, 61f, 79, 87-8, 112, 117,
    126-30
resistance
    political, 83, 104, 137f, 149-50
    therapeutic, 9, 36, 40-1, 60, 105,
retraumatisation, 11, 30, 72
Rohricht, Frank, 128-30
Rosenberg, Jack, 116-17
Rothschild, Babette, 11

self-organisation, 78
self-regulation, 80, 112-14
sensation, 28, 37, 148
sex, sexuality, 7, 30, 34, 38-42, 55-6,
    83, 96
    and power, 143
    and touch, 141-2
    see also gender, heterosexuality,
    queer
Sex-Pol movement, 38
sexual abuse, 13
skying, 106, 108
    see also grounding, centring,
    facing
Social Engagement System (SES),
    73-5, 109, 111
    see also polyvagal theory, Porges,
    Stephen
social theory, 62, 66

Index

sociality, 74-6, 118, 129
society, 37-8, 41, 81-2, 84-5, 104,
    139, 149
socialisation, 12, 29, 100, 140-1
    see also trauma of
Soth, Michael, 69
speech, 17, 39, 74p.
spontaneity, 9, 29, 36-7, 111, 113,
    123
Stern, Daniel, 79-80, 91, 98-9
    see also vitality affect
structural coupling, 78-9, 105
surrender, 9, 41, 52-3, 55, 123-4
sympathetic nervous system, 43,
    73f, 76-7, 106, 110-11
    see also parasympathetic
    nervous system, autonomic
    nervous system

talking therapy, 66
    see also verbal psychotherapy
technologies of the self, 83
Totton, Nick, 3, 7, 9, 15, 17, 28, 44,
    53, 69-70, 79, 85, 108, 133,
    141, 144
touch, therapeutic, 120-2, 141-4,
    148
    see also intricate tactile
    sensitivity
trauma, 9-13, 14, 29-30, 43, 59, 62,
    71-2, 78, 100-1, 107, 117
    and armouring, 101
    and embodiment, 9-13 29, 43,
    62, 117
    and self-regulation, 112-13
    chronic, 10, 100
    of birth, 115
    of socialisation, 12, 100

see also dissociation, fight-flight-
    freeze, retraumatisation
Trauma/Discharge model of body
    psychotherapy, 4, 9-13, 20,
    113
Trevarthen, Colwyn, 79-80
'turn to the body'
    in psychotherapy, 61-2, 66
    in social sciences and
    philosophy, 62, 81-2, 84
'two- person psychotherapy', 67
    see also 'one-person
    psychotherapy'

UK Council for Psychotherapy
    (UKCP), 90
unconscious, 4, 30, 36, 58, 62, 108,
    111-12
    embodied memory, 62
ungroundedness, 8

vagal nerve, 73-4
    see also polyvagal theory
Van der Kolk, Bessel, 62, 117
vegetative
    energy, 42-3, 123
    nervous system, 109
vegetotherapy, 53
verbal psychotherapy, 36-7, 47, 66,
    89, 142-3, 148
    see also talking therapy
viscera, 71, 82, 110
vitality affect, 80, 98-9, 102
    see also Stern, Daniel

Winnicott, DW, 44, 79, 84